Your

Spanish
Vocabulary Guide

for GCSE

John Connor
in association with
Val Levick
Glenise Radford
Alasdair McKeane

Titles available
from
Malvern Language Guides:

French	**German**	**Spanish**	**Italian**
Vocabulary Guide	Vocabulary Guide	Vocabulary Guide	Vocabulary Guide
Speaking Test Guide	Speaking Test Guide	Speaking Test Guide	Speaking Test Guide
Grammar Guide	Grammar Guide	Grammar Guide	Grammar Guide
French Dictionary	German Dictionary		
Mon Echange Scolaire	Mein Austausch	Mi Intercambio Escolar	
Ma Visite En France			
Key Stage 3 Guide	Key Stage 3 Guide	Key Stage 3 Guide	
CE 13+ French			
Standard Grade French			

(Order form inside the back of this book - photocopy and return)

CONTENIDO

Please note the following points:

- Verbs known as "radical changing" verbs, where the vowel in the stem changes, are given with the spelling change in brackets after the infinitive.

  e.g. **encontrar (ue)**

- If an adjective adds **a** to form the feminine or is the same in both masculine and feminine, then only the masculine form is given.

- If an adjective has an irregular feminine form, then the masculine is shown followed by the feminine form.

- Some common words appear in more than one list if they can be used in more than one situation. Page references are made at the end of sections to indicate other words which might be useful to the topic.

AL COLEGIO

La escolariación   School attendance

el   colegio privado ...... prep school
la   escuela .... primary school
el   colegio público ...... (state) school
el   instituto.................. secondary school
el   instituto para alumnos de 16 a 18 años
      .... sixth form college
el   internado..................... boarding school
el   jardín de infancia .... nursery school
la   clase de primer año .... reception class
el   primero de EGB .... year 1 and 2
el   segundo de EGB .... year 3 and 4
el   tercero de EGB .... year 4 and 5
el   cuarto/quinto de EGB ... year 5 and 6
estar en sexto de EGB......... to be in Year 7
estar en séptimo de EGB..... to be in Year 8
estar en octavo de EGB....... to be in Year 9
estar en primero de BUP..... to be in Year 10
estar en segundo de BUP .... to be in Year 11
estar en tercero de BUP ...... to be in Year 12
estar en COU .... to be in Year 13

La gente   People

el   administrador......... bursar
la   administradora .... bursar
el/la alumno(a) .... school boy(girl)
el/la alumno(a) mediopensionista
      .... day-boy/girl
la   amiga.................... (school) friend
el   amigo................... (school) friend
la   caladora .... matron
el/la compañero(a) .... classmate
el/la conserje .... caretaker
el/la director(a) .... headteacher
el/la escolar .... schoolboy/girl
el   interno .... boarder
la   interna .... boarder
el   jefe de estudios ...... student supervisor
la   jefa de estudios ...... student supervisor
el   maestro................. primary school teacher

la   maestra .... primary school teacher
la   pareja.................... partner
el   profesor .... teacher
la   profesora .... teacher
la   secretaria .... secretary

El centro escolar The school complex

el   aula (f).................. classroom
la   biblioteca............... library
la   cafetería................ canteen
el   campo de fútbol..... football pitch
el   centro de documentación ... resources centre
la   enfermería .... sick room
el   gimnasio............... gym
el   laboratorio............. laboratory
la   oficina .... office
el   pasillo................... corridor
el   patio .... playground
la   piscina .... swimming pool
la   pista de tenis .... tennis court
la   residencia .... dormitory
la   sala de profesores .. staffroom
el   salón..................... pupils' common room
el   taller..................... workshop, studio
los vestuarios .... changing rooms

El año escolar   The school year

la   enseñanza .... teaching, education
el   horario.................. timetable
el   intercambio........... school exchange
el   puente................... short break
el   regreso.................. start of school year
la   semana .... week
el   trimestre .... term
las vacaciones a mediados del trimestre
      .... half-term holiday
las vacaciones de verano .... summer holidays
las vacaciones de Navidad.. Christmas holidays
las vacaciones de Pascua.... Easter holidays

1

El día escolar   The school day

el   almuerzo............... midday meal
la   clase .... lesson
los deberes .... homework, prep
el   día .... day
la   hora de comer........ dinner hour
la   lección.................. lesson
la   mañana .... morning
el   recreo .... break
la   reunión .... meeting
la   tarde .... afternoon

El uniforme escolar   School uniform

los calcetines.............. socks
la   camisa .... shirt
la   chaqueta .... blazer
la   corbata.................. tie
la   falda .... skirt
el   jersey.................... pullover
la   rebeca .... cardigan, jumper
los pantalones............. trousers
el   vestido.................. dress
los zapatos................. shoes

For colours see page 28

¿Cómo llegas al colegio?
How do you get to school?

el   autobús .... bus
el   autobús del colegio .... school bus
la   bicicleta .... bicycle
el   coche .... car
el   metro .... underground
el   tranvía .... tram
el   tren .... train

la   estación........................ station
la   estación de autobuses.... bus station
la   estación de metro .... tube station
la   parada de autobuses ...... bus stop

¿A qué hora llegas?
When do you arrive?

puntualmente.............. on time
tarde........................... late
temprano .... early

For clock times see page 91

En la (sala de) clase   In the classroom

el   armario.................. cupboard
los auriculares............. headphones
el   boletín .... report
el   borrador................ duster
la   casilla .... pigeon hole
el   diálogo .... dialogue
el   ejemplo .... example
el   ejercicio................ exercise
el   ensayo .... essay
la   esponja .... sponge
el   magnetofón .... tape recorder
la   mesa...................... table
la   mesa del profesor .. teacher's desk
el   micrófono............. microphone
el   ordenador .... computer
la   pantalla................. screen
la   pared .... wall
el   permiso .... permission
la   pizarra .... (black/white) board
la   puerta .... door
el   pupitre.................. desk
el   retroprojector......... overhead projector
la   silla .... chair
el   suelo..................... floor
el   techo..................... ceiling
la   tiza .... chalk
la   ventana................. window
el   vídeo .... video recorder

la   cita .... extract
los deberes de español. Spanish homework
la   discusión .... debate
la   enseñanza............. education, teaching

el	error.....................	mistake
la	escritura...............	handwriting
la	falta.....................	mistake
la	fila........................	row
la	frase.....................	phrase, sentence
la	gramática..............	grammar
el	idioma..................	language
la	lectura..................	reading
la	letra.....................	handwriting
la	ortografía..............	spelling
la	página..................	page
la	palabra..................	word
el	permiso.................	permission
el	problema...............	problem
el	progreso................	progress, improvement
el	proyecto................	project
la	regla.....................	rule; ruler
la	respuesta...............	reply, answer
el	resultado...............	result
el	resumen................	summary
el	silencio.................	silence
el	símbolo.................	symbol
el	tiempo..................	time
la	traducción.............	translation
el	vocabulario............	vocabulary

El material escolar
Classroom equipment

la	barra de cola..........	glue stick
el	bloc.......................	notepad
el	bolígrafo...............	(ball-point) pen
la	calculadora............	calculator
la	carpeta..................	folder, file, binder
la	cartera..................	school bag
la	chincheta...............	drawing pin
la	cinta adhesiva........	Sellotape®
el	clip.......................	paper clip
la	cola.......................	glue
el	cuaderno...............	exercise book
el	cuaderno de apuntes....	rough book
el	cuadro...................	picture
el	diccionario............	dictionary

el	estuche.................	pencil case
la	goma.....................	rubber
la	grapa.....................	staple
la	grapadora...............	stapler
la	hoja......................	sheet of paper
el	lápiz.....................	pencil
el	libro......................	book
el	libro de apuntes.....	notebook
el	libro de texto........	text book
el	mapa.....................	map
la	mochila.................	rucksack
el	papel (de dibujo)....	(drawing) paper
el	pegamento.............	glue
el	pincel....................	paint brush
la	pluma...................	(fountain) pen
el	punzón..................	hole punch
el	recambio...............	ink cartridge
el	rotulador...............	felt tip pen
el	sacapuntas.............	pencil sharpener
las	tijeras...................	scissors
la	tinta.....................	ink
la	tiza......................	chalk

Las asignaturas   School subjects

el	alemán..................	German
el	arte......................	fine arts
la	biología................	biology
la	cerámica...............	pottery
las	ciencias.................	science
la	cocina...................	cookery
el	comercio...............	business studies
la	costura..................	needlework
el	dibujo...................	drawing
el	drama...................	drama
los	deportes................	sport
la	educación cívica....	PSE
la	educación física.....	physical education
el	español.................	Spanish
la	física....................	physics
el	francés..................	French
la	geografía..............	geography
la	gimnasia...............	gymnastics

3

el	griego	Greek
la	historia	history
el	hogar	home economics
el	idioma moderno	modern language
la	informática	IT, computer studies
el	inglés	English
el	japonés	Japanese
las	lenguas clásicas	classical language
el	latín	Latin
la	literatura	literature
las	matemáticas	maths
la	música	music
la	química	chemistry
la	religión	RE
el	ruso	Russian
la	tecnología	technology
los	trabajos manuales	CDT

Los exámenes   Examinations
Las notas   Marks

el	certificado	certificate, diploma
el	diploma	certificate
el	examen	test paper, exam
la	nota	mark
la	prueba	assessment test
el	resultado	result
el	título	certificate

aprobar (ue)	to pass an exam
examinarse	to take an exam
sacar buenas notas	to get a good mark
sacar malas notas	to get a bad mark
suspender	to fail an exam

El tiempo libre
Out of school activities

la	banda	band
la	charanga	brass band
el	club	club
el	coro	choir
el	equipo	team
la	excursión	trip, outing

el	intercambio	exchange
la	obra de teatro	play
la	orquesta	orchestra
el	partido	match
el	torneo	tournament
la	visita	visit

¿Cómo es?   What is it like?

aburrido(a)	boring
amable	nice
antiguo(a)	old, ex-, former
ausente	absent, away
bueno(a)	good
clásico(a)	classical
complicado(a)	complicated
concienzudo(a)	conscientious
contrario(a)	opposite
correcto(a)	right
de hormigón	of concrete
de ladrillo	of brick
la derecha	right (not left)
difícil	difficult
este(a)	this
estos(as)	these
exacto(a)	exact, precise
excelente	excellent
fácil	easy
fatal	awful
fenomenal	super
flojo(a)	weak, not good at
fuerte	strong, loud, good at
hablador (a)	talkative
incorrecto(a)	wrong
la izquierda	left
simpático(a)	nice
tonto(a)	stupid

bien educado(a)	well-behaved
divertido(a)	amusing, funny
escolar	to do with school
estricto(a)	strict
interesante	interesting

inútil .... not good, hopeless (at)
joven .... young
largo(a) .... long
mediano(a) .... average
mi................................. my
mixto(a) .... mixed
moderno(a) .... modern
nuevo(a) .... new
pasado(a) .... past
perezoso(a) .... lazy
preciso(a)..................... precise
preferido(a) .... favourite
presente .... present, here
privado(a)..................... private
trabajador(a) .... hard-working
travieso(a) .... naughty
último(a)...................... last (final)
útil .... useful
verdad .... true, right
viejo(a) .... old

Adverbios   Adverbs

bien .... well
de prisa........................ quickly
despacio....................... slowly
mal .... badly

Verbos útiles   Useful verbs

abrir............................ to open
aprender .... to learn
apuntar .... to write down
callarse .... to be quiet
completar..................... to complete
contestar .... to reply, answer
copiar .... to copy
corregir....................... to correct
empezar....................... to begin
entender...................... to understand
escoger .... to choose
escribir .... to write
escuchar...................... to listen (to)
estar............................ to be

me gusta...................... I like
hablar.......................... to speak
hacer los deberes .... to do one's homework
hacer una pregunta ...... to ask a question
leer.............................. to read
marcar......................... to tick
oír .... to hear
pedir............................ to ask (for)
repetir.......................... to repeat
ser .... to be

adivinar .... to guess
anotar .... to make notes, note
borrar .... to rub out, erase
calcular........................ to calculate
cantar .... to sing
charlar......................... to chatter
comparar .... to compare
contar .... to count
corresponder............... to correspond
dibujar......................... to draw
discutir .... to discuss
explicar .... to explain
hacer un experimento .. to do an experiment
indicar......................... to point out
levantarse .... to stand up, to get up
mirar .... to look at, watch
mostrar (ue)................. to show
ordenar........................ to put in the right order
preferir .... to prefer
prestar atención .... to be careful, pay
                      attention
recortar........................ to cut out
(re)llenar .... to fill (in); to fill (up)
sentarse .... to sit down
subrayar .... to underline
tachar .... to cross out
torcer........................... to turn
traducir....................... to translate

dar.............................. to give
decir .... to say, tell
dejar............................ to leave

disculparse................... to apologise
durar............................ to last
enseñar........................ to teach
estar equivocado.......... to be wrong
estudiar........................ to study
ir al colegio .... to go to school
jugar (ue)..................... to play (sport)
llegar .... to arrive
llegar tarde .... to be late
llevar .... to wear; to carry
odiar............................ to dislike, hate
olvidarse...................... to forget
pensar.......................... to think
perder .... to lose
poder .... to be able to, can
probar (ue)................... to try (to)
querer .... to want to, wish
saber............................ to know, know how to
salir (de) .... to go out (of)
tener .... to have
tener razón................... to be right

tocar............................ to play (instrument);
　　　　　　　　　　　　　to touch
venir............................ to come
ver............................... to see

aprobar (ue)................. to get a pass mark
aconsejar .... to advise
asistir a........................ to be present at
castigar........................ to punish
copiar........................... to cheat
dejar caer.................... to drop
hacer progresos .... to make progress
hacer tonterías............. to play up, mess about
imaginar...................... to imagine
inventar....................... to invent
parar(se) .... to stop (oneself)
pasar lista .... to call the register
permitir .... to allow, give permission
se trata de .... it is about...
supervisar................... to supervise

For further education and training see page 68

El profesor dice:

Pasad a la sala de clase	Come/go into the classroom
Cierra la puerta/la ventana, por favor	Close the door/the window, please
¡Siéntate/¡Sentaos!	Sit down!
¡Cállate!/¡Callaos!	Quieten down!
¡Levántate/¡Levantaos!	Stand up!
¡Silencio!	Silence!
Voy a pasar lista	I'm going to call the register
Sacad los cuadernos/las carpetas	Get out your exercise books/folders
Coged el libro de español	Pick up your Spanish textbook
Abrid por la página 32	Turn to page 32
Leed el texto	Read the text
Buscad "conejo" en el diccionario	Look up "conejo" in the dictionary
Buscad "conejo" en el vocabulario	Look up "conejo" in the vocabulary
¡Escuchad la cinta!	Listen (to the tape)!
¡Mirad la pantalla/la próxima página!	Look at the screen/the next page!
Repetid	Repeat
Otra vez, todo el mundo	Once more, everyone
Contestad las preguntas	Answer the questions
¿Desde cuándo aprendes el español?	How long have you been learning Spanish?
Mirad la pizarra	Look at the (black/white) board
Escribid la fecha. Es el ocho de setiembre	Put the date. It is September 8th
¿Cuál es la fecha de hoy?/¿A qué día estamos?	What is the date today?
Escribid el título	Put the title
Subrayad con una regla	Use a ruler to underline
Numerad de uno a cinco	Number from one to five
Completad el ejercicio número 2	Finish exercise 2
Completad las frases	Finish the sentences
Corregid el trabajo con un bolígrafo verde	Correct your work with a green pen
Deletrea la palabra "cuaderno"	Spell the word "cuaderno"
Marcad la casilla	Tick the box
¿Verdad o mentira?	True or false?
Escoged la respuesta correcta	Choose the right answer
¡Correcto!	Right!
Cerrad los cuadernos	Shut your exercise books
Pasad los cuadernos a Chris, por favor	Pass the exercise books to Chris, please

Coged los cuadernos .... Pick up the exercise books
Traedme los cuadernos a la sala de profesores, por favor
.... Bring the exercise books to me at the staffroom

Escoge una carta, por favor, Chris .... Choose a card, please, Chris
Escoge a una persona .... Choose someone...
Trabajad en parejas .... Work in pairs
Trabaja con tu pareja .... Work with your partner
Preparad un diálogo .... Work out a dialogue/role play

Copiad los deberes en el cuaderno .... Write down the homework in your exercise books
Es para el martes .... It's for Tuesday
Aprended la lista de vocabulario .... Learn the list of words
Lo haréis para mañana .... You will do it for tomorrow
Es para una prueba el jueves que viene .... There will be a test on it next Thursday
¿Entendéis? .... Do you understand?

¡Cállate!/¡Callaos! .... Stop talking! Be quiet!
¡Daos prisa! .... Hurry up!
¡Guardad las cosas! .... Put your things away!
¡Levantaos! .... Stand up!
Poned las sillas sobre/debajo de las mesas .... Put the chairs on/under the tables
Ven a verme mañana a las nueve .... Come and see me tomorrow morning at 9

El profesor corrige los cuadernos:

Tienes diecisiete sobre veinte .... You got 17 out of 20
Tienes solamente cinco sobre veinte .... You only got 5 out of 20
Hay errores .... There are some mistakes...
"Amarillo" se escribe con elle y una eme .... "Amarillo" is spelt with two l's and one m.
Bastante bien .... Quite good
Bien .... Good
Buen esfuerzo .... Good effort
Muy bien .... Very good
Sobresaliente .... Excellent

Los alumnos dicen:

Estudio el español desde hace un(dos) año(s) .... I've been learning Spanish for one/two years
Entiendo .... I understand
No entiendo .... I don't understand
No sé .... I don't know

Saqué buenas/malas notas............................I got a good/bad mark

¿Hablas español/inglés?............................Do you speak Spanish/English?

Aprendo el español desde hace 2 años ....I have been learning Spanish for 2 years

He olvidado el bolígrafo/el estuche........................I've forgotten my pen/my pencil case

He olvidado los deberes............................I've forgotten my homework

Quiero un cuaderno nuevo, por favor......................I would like a new exercise book, please

Perdón, señorita/señor... ....Please Miss/Sir...

¿En qué página estamos?........................What page are we on?

¿Cómo se dice "homework" en español?................How do you say "homework" in Spanish?

¿Cómo se escribe "el perro"?...................How do you spell "el perro"?

¿Qué significa "el perro" en inglés?......................What does "el perro" mean in English?

¿Cómo se pronuncia eso?......................How do you pronounce that?

¿En qué cuaderno lo hacemos? ....Which exercise book shall we do it in?

¿Quiere repetir eso, por favor?..............Would you say that again, please?

Habla más despacio, por favor..............Would you speak more slowly, please?

¿Puedo abrir la ventana?........................May I open the window?

¿Puedo salir? ....May I leave the room?

¿Puedo sacar punta a mi lápiz? ....May I sharpen my pencil?

Estoy en sexto/séptimo/octavo de EGB..................I am in Year 7/8/9

Estoy en primero/segundo de BUP ....I am in Year 10/11

Algunas frases

Las clases empiezan a las nueve y terminan a las cuatro *Lessons begin at 9 and end at 4*

Tengo seis clases por día *I have six lessons a day*

Mi asignatura preferida es la geografía *My favourite subject is geography*

Se me da bien la historia *I am good at history*

Se me da mal el latín *I am poor at Latin*

Estoy flojo en francés *I'm useless at French*

Voy a examinarme este año *I shall be taking my exams this year*

Llego al colegio a las nueve menos cuarto *I get to school at 8.45 am*

Vengo al colegio a pie *I walk to school*

Llevo uniforme escolar *I wear school uniform*

LA VIDA EN FAMILIA

El alojamiento   Housing

la casa........................ house
la casa adosada .... semi-detached house
la casa separada .... detached house, villa
el edificio .... building
el estudio .... bedsit, studio
la granja .... farm
la manzana .... block of flats
el piso...................... flat
el piso de protección oficial
    .... council, housing association flat

La situación   Situation

las afueras .... suburbs
la aldea .... village
el barrio .... district of town, city
el campo.................... country (not town)
el condado
    ....administrative department (County)
la dirección............... address
el mar....................... sea
el país...................... country (state)
el pueblo................... town; village

el este .... east
el norte .... north
el oeste .... west
el sur .... south

Las señas   Addresses

la avenida .... lane, avenue
la calle...................... street, road
el callejón sin salida... cul de sac
la callejuela .... passage, alley
el camino................... way
la carretera................ main road
el centro .... centre
el muelle................... embankment, quay
el paseo .... boulevard, wide road
la plaza..................... square

el puente................... bridge
el sendero................. lane, path

el alquiler................. rent
el código postal .... postcode
el domicilio.............. home
el dueño .... owner
el número................. number
el número de teléfono....... phone number
la vista...................... view

Palabras generales General

el ascensor................ lift
el balcón................... balcony
la bienvenida............ welcome
la chimenea.............. fireplace, chimney
la entrada.................. entrance
la escalera................. staircase
el estante .... shelf, stand
el inquilino............... tenant
la llave .... key
la limpieza................ cleaning
la luz .... light
el mango .... handle
el metro cuadrado...... square metre
la pared .... wall
el pasillo................... corridor
el peldaño................. step (on stairs)
la pintura.................. paint(ing)
el piso .... floor, storey
el plano .... plan
la puerta .... gate
la puerta principal...... (front) door
el rellano .... landing
el suelo..................... floor
el techo..................... ceiling
la ventana................. window

el agua...................... water
la barandilla .... banisters
la bombilla .... light bulb

10

la calefacción central . central heating
la cerradura............... lock
la contraventana........ shutter
el cristal.................... glass
la electricidad .... electricity
el enchufe (hembra) ... socket
el enchufe (macho) .... plug
el gas....................... gas
los habitantes.............. inhabitants
el interruptor............. switch
el primer piso .... first floor, upstairs
la planta baja .... ground floor
el radiador .... radiator
el techo.................... roof
el vidrio.................... glass

Las habitaciones   Rooms

el aseo .... toilet
el ático...................... attic, loft
la cocina .... kitchen
el comedor................ dining room
el cuarto de baño .... bathroom
el cuarto de estar........ living-room
el cuarto de los niños .... playroom
el despacho............... study
el desván................... attic, loft
el dormitorio............. bedroom
el garaje.................... garage
el invernadero........... conservatory
el sótano .... cellar
el salón .... living-room, lounge
el servicio .... toilet
la terraza................... terrace
la trascocina.............. utility room
el vestíbulo .... hall

El cuarto de baño   Bathroom
el agua caliente.......... hot water
el agua fría................ cold water
el aseo .... toilet
el baño de espuma ..... bubble bath
la bañera................... bath (tub)

el baño .... bath (activity);
                           bathroom
el bidé .... bidet
el cepillo de dientes ... toothbrush
el champú................. shampoo
el desodorante .... deodorant
la ducha.................... shower
el espejo .... mirror
la esponja .... sponge
el grifo .... tap
el jabón .... soap
el lavabo................... wash basin
la maquinilla de afeitar ... razor
la pasta de dientes...... toothpaste
el paño .... flannel
la toalla .... towel
la toalla de baño .... bath towel

El dormitorio   Bedroom
el armario................. wardrobe
la cadena estereofónica ... music centre
el casete................... cassette
el cepillo .... brush
el compacto.............. compact disc
el edredón................. duvet, quilt
el espejo .... mirror
la funda del edredón .. duvet cover
la manta................... blanket
la sábana................... sheet
la silla...................... chair
el videojuego............ video game
el walkman® .... personal stereo

la alfombra............... rug, carpet (not fitted)
la almohada.............. pillow
la cama.................... bed
la cortina .... curtain
la despertador........... radio clock
los juguetes .... toys
la lámpara................. lamp
el libro..................... book
la moqueta............... fitted carpet
el ordenador .... computer

el	peine	comb
el	póster	poster
el	secador de pelo	hairdryer
el	televisor	television set

El cuarto de estar — Living room/Lounge

el	cenicero	ashtray
la	chimenea	fireplace
el	cojín	cushion
el	disco compacto	compact disc
el	equipo de discos compactos	CD player
el	equipo de alta fidelidad	music centre
la	foto	photo
la	librería	book-case
el	magnetofón	cassette recorder
la	mesita	coffee table
la	moqueta	fitted carpet
el	piano	piano
la	pintura	painting
el	reloj	clock
el	sillón	armchair
el	sofá	sofa, settee
la	televisión	television
el	televisor	TV set
el	vídeo	video recorder

El comedor — Dining room

el	aparador	sideboard
la	cafetera	coffee pot
la	copa	(wine) glass
el	cuadro	picture
la	cuchara	spoon
el	cuchillo	knife
el	mantel	tablecloth
la	mesa	table
el	platito	saucer
el	plato	plate
el	sacacorchos	corkscrew
la	silla	chair
la	taza	cup
el	tazón	bowl
el	tenedor	fork

la	tetera	teapot
la	vajilla	crockery
el	vaso	glass (for water)
la	vela	candle

La cocina — Kitchen

el	abrebotellas	bottle opener
el	abrelatas	can opener
el	armario	cupboard
la	aspiradora	vacuum cleaner
la	bandeja	tray
la	basura	rubbish bin
la	cacerola	saucepan
la	cazuela	casserole
las	cerillas	matches
la	cocina de gas	gas cooker
la	cocina eléctrica	electric cooker
el	congelador	freezer
el	fregadero	sink
el	frigorífico	fridge
el	horno	oven
la	lavadora	washing machine
el	lavaplatos	dishwasher
el	microondas	microwave
la	nevera	fridge
la	olla a presión	pressure cooker
la	plancha	iron
la	sartén	frying pan
la	secadora	tumble dryer
la	tabla de planchar	ironing board
la	tetera	kettle
el	tostador	toaster

El vestíbulo — Hall

el	contestador automático	answering machine
la	entrada	entrance
la	escalera	staircase
la	llave	key
la	puerta principal	front door
el	teléfono	telephone

El garaje	Garage
el automóvil	car
la bici(cleta)	bike
el coche	car
el cortacésped	lawnmower
las herramientas	tools
la motocicleta	motorbike

El jardín	Garden
el abeto	fir tree
el aparcamiento	parking space
el árbol frutal	(fruit) tree
el arbusto	shrub
la carretilla	wheelbarrow
el césped	lawn
el cobertizo	shed
la flor	flower
la fruta	fruit
la hierba	grass
el huerto	vegetable garden
el invernáculo	greenhouse
la legumbre	vegetable
el macizo	flower bed
el manzano	apple tree
el seto	hedge
la terraza	terrace, patio

¿Cómo es?	What is it like?
acogedor(a)	welcoming
amable	pleasant
arriba	upstairs, above
bonito(a)	pretty
caro(a)	dear, expensive
cómodo(a)	comfortable
de lujo	luxurious, posh
elegante	smart
empotrado(a)	fitted, converted
en buenas condiciones	in good condition
en malas condiciones	in poor condition
esencial	essential
estrecho(a)	narrow
feo(a)	ugly
flamante	brand new

grande	big
hermoso(a)	beautiful
limpio(a)	clean
lujoso(a)	luxurious, posh
necesario(a)	necessary
nuevo(a)	new
pequeño(a)	small
perfecto(a)	perfect
práctico(a)	practical
privado(a)	private
propio(a)	own
raro(a)	odd, strange
ruidoso(a)	noisy
sucio(a)	dirty
tranquilo(a)	quiet, peaceful
vacio(a)	empty
antiguo(a)	old, ex-, former
industrial	industrial
pintoresco(a)	picturesque
turista	tourist
típico(a)	typical

¿Dónde está?	Where is it?
da a la calle	overlooks the street
da al jardín	overlooks the garden
abajo	downstairs, below
arriba	upstairs
en la planta baja	on the ground floor
en	in, on
entre	between
debajo de	under
delante de	in front of
detrás de	behind
por allí	that way
por aquí	this way

Verbos útiles	Useful verbs
abrir	to open, turn on the tap
apagar	to switch off
arreglar	to tidy up
ayudar	to help

cocinar......................... to do the cooking

compartir..................... to share

comprar....................... to buy

encender (ie).............. to light, switch on

enjugar .... to wipe

fregar (ie) .... to do the washing up

hacer la cama.............. to make the bed

hacer la compra .... to do the shopping

hacer las tareas domésticas . to do housework

lavar la ropa................. to do the washing

limpiar......................... to clean

necesitar .... to need

planchar la ropa........... to iron clothes

poner el gas .... to turn on the gas

poner la mesa .... to set the table

poner la radio .... to switch on the radio

preparar la comida....... to get meals ready

quitar la mesa .... to clear the table

reparar......................... to repair

trabajar en el jardín...... to garden

vivir.............................. to live, reside

amueblar...................... to furnish

cerrar........................... to shut, turn off tap

cortar el césped............ to mow the lawn

dar la bienvenida .... to greet, welcome

decorar .... to decorate

enchufar .... to plug in

ensanchar..................... to extend

hacer bricolaje............. to do odd jobs, DIY

llamar (a la puerta) ...... to knock on the door

modificar..................... to convert

mudarse....................... to move house

pasar la aspiradora....... to vacuum

regar (ie)..................... to water

revolcar (ue)............... to upset, overturn

tocar (el timbre) .... to ring (the doorbell)

acostarse (ue) .... to go to bed

adormecerse .... to fall asleep

afeitarse...................... to shave

almorzar (ue).............. to have lunch

beber .... to drink

cenar .... to have evening meal

cepillar el pelo............. to brush one's hair

comer........................... to eat

desayunar .... to have breakfast

despertarse (ie)............ to wake up

lavarse......................... to wash oneself

levantarse .... to get up

limpiarse los dientes.... to clean one's teeth

peinarse el pelo .... to comb one's hair

tener hambre .... to be hungry

tener sed...................... to be thirsty

vestirse (i) .... to get dressed

dejar............................ to leave

encontrar .... to meet, find

entrar........................... to go into

llegar a .... to arrive at

salir de .... to go out of

For meals see page 23

For food and drink see page 53

For pets see page 29

For weekend activities and hobbies see page 31

For expressing opinions see page 38

For colours see page 28

For times see page 91

Algunas frases

¿Dónde vives? *Where do you live?*

¿Qué hay en tu dormitorio? *What is there in your bedroom?*

¿Qué hay en tu jardín? *What is there in your garden?*

Vivo en la planta baja *I live on the ground floor*

Mi hermano lleva al perro de paseo *My brother takes the dog for a walk*

Friego los platos *I do the washing up*

Ser invitado   **Being a guest**

el   amigo de intercambio.. penfriend

la   huéspeda............... hostess

el   huésped................ host

la   invitada................ guest

el   invitado............... guest

el   cepillo de dientes ... toothbrush

el   champú................. shampoo

el   jabón.................... soap

la   maleta.................. suitcase

la   manta................... blanket

la   pasta de dientes...... toothpaste

el   regalo................... present

acogedor(a)................. welcoming

amable........................ kind

encantado(a)............... pleased

francés(a)................... French

inglés(a) .... English

interesante .... interesting

mayor........................ elder, oldest

menor........................ younger, youngest

simpático(a)............... nice

tímido(a) .... shy

viejo(a)....................... aged, elderly

For nationalities see pages 29 and 88

Verbos útiles   **Useful verbs**

ayudar .... to help

comer........................ to eat

dar .... to give (present)

dar la bienvenida .... to welcome

dejar.......................... to leave

encontrar (ue) .... to find

entrar........................ to come in

estar situado .... to be situated

hablar francés............. to speak French

hablar inglés............... to speak English

llegar......................... to arrive

necesitar.................... to need

olvidar(se) .... to forget

pedir prestado............. to borrow

poder......................... to be able to

prestar .... to lend

salir .... to go out

sonreír .... to smile

Algunas frases

He olvidado un paño *I have forgotten a flannel*

¿Dónde está el cuarto de baño? *Where is the bathroom, please?*

¿Puedo llamar a mi padre, por favor? *May I phone my father, please?*

Cenamos sobre las ocho de la tarde *We have our evening meal at about 8 pm*

LOS MEDIOS DE COMUNICACIÓN

Palabras generales General

el cine........................ cinema
la prensa.................... press
la radio...................... radio
el teatro..................... theatre
la televisión.............. television

En el cine **At the cinema**

el actor...................... actor
la actriz...................... actress
el argumento.............. plot
la estrella................... filmstar
la función de tarde..... afternoon performance
el malo....................... baddie, villain
la película.................. film
el personaje.............. character
el programa............... programme
el protagonista.......... hero/heroine
la sesión.................... (film) showing
los subtítulos.............. subtitles

¿Qué ponen? **What's on?**

la comedia................. comedy film
los dibujos animados... cartoon
la película de amor.... love film
la película de aventuras... adventure film
la película de ciencia ficción
.... science fiction film
la película de espionaje..... spy film
la película de guerra......... war film
la película de suspense...... thriller
la película de terror.... horror film
la película policíaca... detective film
el western.................. Western

La prensa **The press**

el lector..................... reader
el quiosco.................. news stand
el vendedor de periódicos. newsagent

los anuncios............... small ads

el artículo................. article
los crucigramas.......... crosswords
el diario..................... daily paper
la lectura.................. reading
la página deportiva.... sports page
el periódico.............. newspaper
el pronóstico del tiempo. weather report
el reportaje............... report
la revista................... magazine
la revista de aventuras.... adventure magazine
la revista de moda..... fashion magazine
la revista de mujeres.. women's magazine
la revista de noticias.. news magazine
la revista ilustrada..... illustrated magazine
el semanal................ weekly paper, magazine
la tira cómica............ comic strip
los titulares................ headlines

En la radio **On the radio**
En la televisión **On TV**

el cantante................ singer (female)
la cantante................ singer (male)
la cómica.................. comedienne
el cómico.................. comedian
el grupo.................... group
el pronóstico del tiempo......weather forecast
el programa de entrevistas...a talk show

la antena parabólica... satellite dish
los anuncios............... adverts
el canal..................... channel
la cinta de vídeo........ video cassette
el concurso............... quiz
el culebrón............... serial
los deportes................ sports broadcast
el documental........... documentary
la emisión................. broadcast
el mando a distancia.. remote control, zapper
la obra de teatro......... play
la revista................... variety programme

16

la	serie policíaca	detective, police series
el	telediario	TV news
la	telenovela	"soap"
la	televisión por cable	cable TV
el	vídeo	VCR

La música   Music

la	cadena estereofónica ...	stereo system
el	cantante	singer (female)
la	cantante	singer (male)
el	disco compacto	compact disc, CD
el	equipo de discos compactos	CD player
el	jazz	jazz
el	magnetofón	cassette recorder
la	música clásica	classical music
la	música pop	pop music
el	rap	rap
el	rock	rock
el	walkman®	personal stereo

El teatro   The theatre

el	argumento	plot
la	audiencia	audience
el	ballet	ballet
la	comedia	comedy
la	compañía	theatre company
el	drama	drama
la	obra	play
el	ópera	opera
la	representación	performance
la	tragedia	tragedy

¿Cuándo lo viste/oíste?
When did you see/hear it?

(por la) mañana	(in the) morning
(por la) tarde	(in the) afternoon
(por la) tarde	(in the) evening
en el fin de semana	at the weekend
anteayer	the day before
ayer	yesterday
esta mañana	this morning
hace tres días	three days ago

hace un mes	a month ago
hoy	today
la semana pasada	last week

¿Dónde lo viste/oíste?
Where did you see/hear it?

en la radio	on the radio
en el cine	at the cinema
en el club de jóvenes ...	at the youth club
en el concierto	at a concert
en el teatro..................	at the theatre
en la televisión	on television
en vídeo......................	on video

¿Cómo es?   What is it like?

aburrido(a)	boring
agradable....................	nice
bien	well, good
bueno(a)	good
fatal............................	awful
clásico(a)	classical
corto(a)	short
desagradable...............	unpleasant, painful
diario(a)	daily
divertido(a)	funny, amusing
doblado(a)	dubbed
emocionante	exciting
estupendo(a)	super
excelente	excellent
extraordinario(a)..........	extraordinary, special
famoso(a)	famous
favorito(a)	favourite
gracioso(a)	funny
impresionante.............	impressive
interesante	interesting
inútil...........................	useless
joven	young
largo(a)	long
malo(a)........................	bad
mensual......................	monthly
muy bueno(a)	very good, super
(no) malo(a)	(not) bad
normalmente	usually

pop .... pop
preferido(a) .... favourite
ridículo(a) .... ridiculous
semanal .... weekly
sensacional .... sensational
serio(a) .... serious
subtitulado(a) .... sub-titled
terrible......................... ugly, horrible, lousy
trágico(a) .... tragic
último(a) .... last, latest
versión española .... in the Spanish version
versión original............ with the original
soundtrack

Verbos útiles   **Useful verbs**
apagar, cerrar.............. to switch off, close
apreciar .... to appreciate
cambiar de canal......... to channel-hop
cantar .... to sing
comparar .... to compare
desdeñar .... to despise
durar........................... to last
empezar....................... to begin
encontrar .... to find
escoger .... to choose
escuchar .... to listen (to)
grabar .... to record

gustar(impers.) .... to like
gustar mucho.............. to like a lot
interesarse en.............. to be interested in
ir a ver........................ to go and see
leer............................. to read
llamar por teléfono ...... to phone
mirar .... to watch
(no) gustar.................. not to like, dislike
odiar........................... to hate
oír .... to hear
pasarlo bien................ to have a good time
pensar......................... to think
poder.......................... to be able to, can
poner.......................... to switch on
preferir .... to prefer
reír .... to laugh
se trata de................... it is about
terminar...................... to end
tocar........................... to play
ver .... to see

For words to express an opinion see pages 38, 40
For days of the week see page 92
For buying tickets see page 34
For advertising see page74

Algunas frases

¿Vamos al cine? *Shall we go to the cinema?*

¿Qué ponen? *What's on?*

Me gustan las comedias *I like comic films*

Me gusta escuchar música *I like listening to music*

Me interesa el jazz *I'm interested in jazz*

Tengo una colección de discos compactos *I have a collection of CDs*

¿Qué tal lo encontraste? *What did you think of it?*

¿Dónde lo viste? *Where did you see it?*

¿Dónde lo escuchaste? *Where did you hear it?*

LA SALUD Y LA FORMA FÍSICA

Las partes de cuerpo
Parts of the body

la barbilla .... chin
la boca .... mouth
el brazo .... arm
la cabeza .... head
la cadera .... hip
la cara .... face
el cerebro .... brain
la cintura .... waist
el codo .... elbow
el corazón .... heart
la costilla .... rib
el cuello .... neck
el dedo .... finger
el dedo del pie .... toe
el diente .... tooth
la espalda .... back
el estómago .... stomach
las facciones .... features
la frente .... forehead
la garganta .... throat
el hígado .... liver
el hombro .... shoulder
el hueso .... bone
el labio .... lip
la lengua .... tongue
la mano .... hand
la mejilla .... cheek
el miembro .... limb
la muñeca .... wrist
el músculo .... muscle
el muslo .... thigh
la nariz .... nose
la nuca .... nape of neck
el ojo .... eye
la oreja .... ear
el pecho .... chest, bust
los pechos .... breasts
el pelo .... hair

el pie .... foot
la piel .... skin
la pierna .... leg
el pulgar .... thumb
el pulmón .... lungs
el riñón .... kidneys
la rodilla .... knee
la sangre .... blood
el tobillo .... ankle
la uña .... finger nail
el vientre .... stomach, tummy
la voz .... voice

La gente   People

el/la asistente social ..... social worker
el/la dentista .... dentist
el/la doctor(a) .... doctor
el/la enfermero(a) .... nurse
el/la enfermo(a) .... patient
el/la farmacéutico(a).... chemist
el/la fisioterapeuta .... physiotherapist
el/la médico(a) .... doctor
el/la óptico(a) .... optician
el/la psicólogo(a) .... psychologist
el/la psiquiatra .... psychiatrist

Problemas de salud Health problems

la amigdalitis .... tonsillitis
la diarrea .... diarrhoea
el dolor de cabeza ...... headache
la fiebre .... fever, high temperature
la fiebre del heno .... hay fever
la gripe .... flu
la hinchazón .... swelling
la indigestión .... indigestion
la insolación .... sunstroke
el mareo .... sea-sickness
la mordedura .... bite
las paperas .... mumps
la picadura .... (insect) sting, bite

19

la regla .... period
el resfriado .... cold
la rubeola.................. German measles
el sarampión .... measles
la torcedura............... sprain
la tos........................... cough
la varicela................... chicken pox

En el médico y en el dentista
At the doctor's and the dentist's

la ambulancia .... ambulance
el certificado médico . doctor's certificate
la cirugía .... surgery
la cita........................ appointment
la clínica................... clinic
el consultorio............ surgery
el dolor...................... pain
el empaste................. filling
la enfermedad........... illness
la escayola................ plaster (broken bones)
las gafas..................... spectacles
los gastos.................... expenses, cost
la inyección .... injection
la medicina............... medicine, treatment
la operación.............. operation
los primeros auxilios ... first aid
el problema............... problem
los rayos X.................. X-ray
la receta..................... prescription
el remedio .... remedy
el seguro................... insurance
el tratamiento............ treatment
la vez........................ time, occasion

En la farmacia   At the chemist's

el algodón................. cotton wool
los antibióticos .... antibiotics
la aspirina................. aspirin
la compresa .... sanitary towel
el comprimido .... tablet
la crema.................... cream
la cucharada.............. spoonful

el jabón .... soap
el jarabe .... (liquid) medicine, cough mixture
el pañuelo de papel.... tissue
la pasta de dientes...... toothpaste
la pastilla para la garganta ...throat sweet
la quemadura del sol.. sunburn
el supositorio............ suppository
el tampón .... tampon
el vendaje................. dressing
la fiebre.................... temperature
la tirita..................... plaster, elastoplast®
el tubo...................... tube

Verbos útiles   Useful verbs

aconsejar .... to advise
acostarse (ue) .... to go to bed
disculparse .... to apologize
doler el estómago .... to have stomach-ache
doler la cabeza............. to have a headache
doler la espalda .... to have backache
doler la garganta.......... to have a sore throat
doler el oído .... to have earache
doler los dientes .... to have toothache
dormir(se) (ue) .... to sleep
esperar........................ to wait (for)
estar mareado(a) .... to feel sick
estar preocupado(a) ..... to be worried
estornudar .... to sneeze
guardar cama.............. to stay in bed
hacer una cita .... to make an appointment
herirse .... to get injured
informar .... to inform
ir a ver........................ to go and see
llamar......................... to call
morder .... to bite
pagar .... to pay (for)
picar........................... to sting, to inject
ponerse....................... to become
relajar(se) .... to relax
rellenar....................... to fill
sentirse bien .... to feel well

sentirse mal .... to feel ill
sudar .... to sweat
ser admitido(a) al hospital
 .... to be admitted to hospital
ser alérgico(a) a .... to be allergic to
tener calor .... to be hot
tener fiebre .... to have a raised temperature
tener frío .... to be cold
tener miedo .... to be afraid
tener sueño .... to be sleepy
tener un resfriado .... to have a cold
tiritar .... to shiver
tomar la temperatura a alguien
 .... to take someone's temperature
toser .... to cough
vomitar .... to vomit

Un estilo de vida sano
A healthy lifestyle

el aerobic .... aerobics
la agricultura orgánica ...... organic farming
el alcohol .... alcohol
los alimentos .... food
los alimentos orgánicos ...... organic foods
las anfetaminas .... amphetamines
la anorexia .... anorexia
la (buena) forma física ...... fitness
la bulimia .... bulimia
el contenido de grasa . fat content
la droga .... drug
el drogadicto .... junkie
los dulces .... sweet things
la embriaguez .... drunkenness (habitual)
el entrenamiento diario .... daily work-out
el esnifador de pegamento .. glue sniffer
el estrés .... stress
el fertilizante químico ....chemical fertiliser
la fruta .... fruit
el fumador .... smoker
    gordo(a) .... fat
las grasas .... fats

la heroína .... heroin
la hipertensión .... high blood pressure
la industria de comida rápida
 .... fast food industry
el insecticida .... insecticide
las legumbres .... vegetables
los productos lácteos ... dairy products
el SIDA .... Aids
la sobredosis .... overdose
el sueño .... sleep
el tabaco .... tobacco
el toxicómano .... drug addict
las vitaminas .... vitamins

¿Qué pasa?   What's the matter?

anoréxico(a) .... anorexic
borracho(a) .... drunk
caliente .... hot
cansado(a) .... tired
cierto(a) .... certain, sure
débil .... weak
diabético(a) .... diabetic
enfermo(a) ill
estar resfriado(a) .... having a cold
frío(a) .... cold
grueso(a) .... fat, fatty
hinchado(a) .... swollen
indispuesto(a) .... unwell
limpio(a) .... clean
lo siento mucho .... very sorry
minusválido(a) .... handicapped
mojado(a) .... wet
sano(a) .... healthy
seguro(a) .... certain
sorprendente .... surprising
sucio(a) .... dirty
urgente .... urgent
vegetariano(a) .... vegetarian
vegetariano(a) estricto(a) .... vegan
verdadero(a) .... true

Verbos útiles　　Useful verbs

adelgazar .... to lose weight
comer .... to eat
descansar .... to rest
drogarse....................... to take drugs
enfadarse .... to get angry
engordar .... to put on weight
entrenar(se) .... to train
estar agotado(a) .... to be exhausted
estar bien de salud .... to be in good health
estar en buena forma.... to be very fit
estar mal de salud .... to be in poor health
evitar .... to avoid
fumar.......................... to smoke
ir más despacio............ to slow down
lavar .... to wash
levantar(se)................. to get up
mirar .... to watch, look at
parar(se) .... to stop
ponerse a régimen........ to go on a diet
prestar atención .... to pay attention
probar la droga .... to try drugs
protestar .... to protest
sangrar........................ to bleed
tener respeto a .... to have respect for

¿Es grave?　　Is it serious?

agotado(a) .... exhausted
arrepentido(a) .... sorry, regretful

conmocionado(a) .... in shock
falso(a) .... false, wrong
grave .... serious
gravemente herido(a)... seriously injured
herido(a) .... injured
despacio .... slowly
inconsciente .... unconscious
muerto(a) .... dead
preocupado(a) .... worried, anxious

Verbos útiles　　Useful verbs

adelantar..................... to overtake
ayudar .... to help
correr .... to run
cortarse el dedo .... to cut one's finger
darse prisa .... to hurry
declarar .... to declare
gritar .... to shout
hacerse daño............... to hurt oneself
llorar .... to cry (weep)
matar.......................... to kill
perdonar..................... to forgive
quemar .... to burn
quemarse la mano........ to burn one's hand
romperse el brazo........ to break one's arm
torcerse el tobillo........ to sprain one's ankle

For sport etc see page 33
For food and drink see pages 53, 23

Algunas frases

¿Qué pasa? *What is the matter?*
Me he roto la pierna *I've broken my leg*
Tengo mucha fiebre *I've got a high temperature*
Le ha picado un mosquito *A mosquito has stung him*
Estoy mareado *I feel sick*
¿Tiene algo para la tos? *Have you anything for a cough?*

COMER Y BEBER

Las comidas   Meals

el	almuerzo	lunch, midday meal
la	cena	dinner, evening meal
la	comida	food
la	comida para llevar	take-away meals
el	desayuno	breakfast
la	merienda	afternoon tea, snack
el	picnic	picnic
el	piscolabis	snack

¿Dónde vas a comer?
Where are you going to eat?

el	bar	bar
la	cafetería	café
la	pizzería	pizzeria
el	restaurante	restaurant
el	restaurante autoservicio	self-service restaurant
el	restaurante de comida rápida	fast food restaurant

En un restaurante   In a restaurant

La gente   People

el/la	cajero(a)	till operator
la	camarera	waitress
el	camarero	waiter
el/la	cliente	customer
el/la	cocinero(a)	chef
el/la	dueño(a)	owner
la	persona	person

Palabras generales   General

afuera		outside
dentro		inside
en la terraza		on the terrace
(no) incluido		(not) included

la	bandeja	tray
la	comida china	Chinese food
la	comida francesa	French food

la	comida india	Indian food
la	cuenta	bill
la	especialidad (de la región)	(local) speciality
el	menú del día	menu of the day
la	mesa	table
el	olor	smell
el	plato del día	dish of the day
el	precio del cubierto	cover charge
la	propina	tip
la	receta	recipe
el	recibo	receipt
el	sabor	flavour, taste
la	selección	choice
el	servicio	service charge
los	servicios	toilets
la	silla	chair
el	teléfono	telephone

El menú   Menu

el	entremés	starter, entrée
la	especialidad del día	the day's "special"
el	pescado	fish
el	plato principal	main course
el	postre	dessert
el	queso	cheese

Los entremeses   Starters

el	caldo	consommé
el	chorizo	red hard sausage
la	ensalada de tomate	tomato salad
los	fiambres variados	mixed cold meats
el	gazpacho	cold soup
las	verduras crudas	chopped raw vegetables
el	paté	pâté
la	sopa	soup
la	sopa de cebolla	onion soup

El plato principal   Main course

el	bistec y las patatas fritas	steak and chips
la	chuleta de cerdo	pork chop
el	crep	savoury pancake

el   escalope de ternera........ veal escalope
el   guiso...................... casserole
el   pato a la naranja..... duck in orange sauce
la   pizza..................... pizza
el   pollo al vino tinto .. chicken in red wine
el   surtido de tortilla ... choice of omelettes

Postre   **Dessert**
el   flan........................ creme caramel
el   helado (casero) ...... (home made) ice cream
el   helado de chocolate..... chocolate ice cream
el   helado de vainilla... vanilla ice cream
el   mousse de chocolate ...chocolate mousse
la   nata........................ whipped cream
las pastas..................... cake, pastry
el   pastel .... gâteau
el   queso (de cabra)..... (goat's) cheese
la   tarta de manzana.... apple tart
la   tortita.................... pancake
el   yogur .... yoghurt

En la mesa   **On the table**
la   botella.................... bottle
la   cafetera................. coffee pot
la   cuchara .... spoon
el   cuchillo................. knife
la   jarra...................... carafe (water, wine)
el   mantel.................... tablecloth
la   mostaza................. mustard
el   pimiento .... pepper
el   platito .... saucer
el   plato .... plate
la   sal......................... salt
la   taza....................... cup
el   tazón..................... bowl
el   tenedor................. fork
el   vaso...................... glass

En la cafetería   At the café
Las bebidas   **Drinks**
el   agua...................... water
el   agua mineral (con gas)
     .... (sparkling) mineral water
el   aperitivo .... pre-meal drink, aperitif
el   batido de chocolate.... chocolate milk shake
el   café .... filter coffee
el   café con leche........ white coffee
el   café solo .... coffee (black)
la   cerveza .... beer
el   chocolate .... hot chocolate
la   coca cola®............ coca cola®
el   cubito de hielo....... ice cube
la   limonada............... lemonade
la   sidra .... cider
el   té.......................... tea
el   vino blanco........... white wine
el   vino tinto.............. red wine
el   zumo de fruta .... fruit juice
el   zumo de limón....... fresh lemon juice

Un piscolabis   **A snack**
el   bocadillo de jamón ....ham sandwich
el   bocadillo de queso .....cheese sandwich
el   bollo..................... doughnut
los churros .... deep-fried sticks of
                               sweet batter
el   gofre..................... waffle
la   hamburguesa .... hamburger
el   helado................... ice cream
las patatas fritas .... crisps, chips
la   tortita................... pancake

Exclamaciones   **Exclamations**
¡Basta!......................... That is enough!
¡Bravo!........................ Well done!
¡Felicitaciones!........... Congratulations!
¡(no) gracias!.............. (no) thank you!
¡Buen aprovecho .... Enjoy your meal!
¡Que aproveche(n)....... Enjoy your meal!
¡Salud! .... Cheers!
por favor .... please

Verbos útiles — Useful verbs

almorzar (ue)	to have lunch
beber	to drink
cenar	to have dinner
comer	to eat
costar (ue)	to cost
desayunar	to have breakfast
desear	to wish, want
encantar	to love
escoger	to choose
gustar	to like, to please
gustar mucho	to love
odiar	to hate
ofrecer	to offer
pasar	to pass
pedir	to order
preferir (ie)	to prefer
quejarse (de)	to complain
querer (ie)	to want (to)
recomendar (ie)	to recommend
reservar	to reserve
servir (i)	to serve
tener hambre/sed	to be hungry/thirsty
tomar	to take
traer	to bring

For festivals see page 43

For recipe words see page 55

For national and special foods see page 80

For lists of fruit, vegetables, fish, meat and general foodstuffs see page 53

For money and prices see pages 76, 56

For weights and measures see page 56

Algunas frases

Tengo hambre *I'm hungry*

Tengo sed *I'm thirsty*

¿Tiene una mesa para dos personas? *Have you a table for two?*

Tengo una mesa reservada en nombre de Smith *I've booked a table in the name of Smith*

El menú, por favor *May I have the menu, please?*

¿Puede explicarme lo que es la "fabada"? *Please can you explain what "fabada" is?*

Quisiera pedir *I would like to order*

Voy a tomar el menú de mil quininentas pesetas *I'll have the 1500 peseta menu*

Para empezar voy a tomar la sopa de cebolla *For starter, I'll have onion soup*

No me gustan las judías verdes *I don't like green beans*

De postre voy a tomar el mousse de chocolate *For dessert, I'll have chocolate mousse*

Un poco más de pan, por favor *May we have more bread, please?*

¿Puede hacer el favor de cambiarme este vaso? *Will you change this glass, please?*

Necesitamos otro tenedor *We need another fork*

La cuenta por favor *May I have the bill, please?*

¿Está incluido el servicio? *Is service included?*

¿Dónde están los servicios por favor? *Where is the toilet, please?*

¿Se puede telefonear desde aquí? *May we phone from here?*

MI FAMILIA, MIS AMIGOS, YO MISMO(A)

Palabras generales General

La dirección　Address
la calle..................... street
el código postal .... postcode
la dirección............... address
el lugar de residencia........ place of residence
el número de fax.............. fax number
el número de teléfono....... phone number
el pueblo................... town; village

La identidad　Identity
el apellido................. surname
el apodo.................... nickname
el carnet de identidad.....identity card
la documentación....... proof of identity
la estatura................. height
la fecha de nacimiento ...date of birth
la firma.................... signature
la identidad............... identity
el lugar de nacimiento ...place of birth
el nombre .... (first) name
el pasaporte .... passport
　Señor.................... Mr
　Señora .... Mrs, Ms
　Señorita .... Miss

La edad　Age
el año........................ year
el cumpleaños............ birthday
la edad..................... age
la fecha.................... date
el mes...................... month
el nacimiento............ birth
la vejez.................... old age
la vida .... life

La familia y los amigos
Family and friends

La familia　Close family
la cuñada .... sister-in-law
el cuñado.................. brother-in-law

la hermana................ sister
el hermano .... brother
la hija...................... daughter
la hijastra.................. stepdaughter
el hijastro .... stepson
el hijo...................... son
la madrastra.............:.. stepmother
la madre .... mother
　mamá .... mummy
el marido.................. husband
la media hermana ...... half sister
el medio hermano...... half brother
la mujer.................... wife
el padrastro............... stepfather
el padre .... father
los padres................... parents
　papá..................... daddy

Otros parentes　Other relatives
la abuela................... grandmother
el abuelo.................. grandfather
los abuelos .... grandparents
la nieta .... granddaughter
el nieto .... grandson
la nuera .... daughter-in-law
los parientes............... relatives
el primo.................... cousin
la prima.................... cousin
la sobrina.................. niece
el sobrino .... nephew
la suegra................... mother-in-law
el suegro................... father-in-law
la tía........................ aunt
el tío........................ uncle
el yerno.................... son-in-law

La gente　People
el adolescente............ teenager
el adulto .... adult
la amiga .... friend (girl)
el amigo .... friend (boy)

el bebé .... baby
el caballero .... gentleman
la chica .... girl
el chico .... boy
el amigo de intercambio .. penfriend
la dama .... lady
la divorciada .... divorced woman
el divorciado .... divorced man
el/la extranjero(a) .... foreigner; stranger
las gemelas .... twins (girls)
los gemelos .... twins (boys, mixed)
la generación más joven/menor
.... the younger generation
la generación más vieja/mayor
.... the older generation
la gente .... people
el hombre .... man
los jubilados .... senior citizens
la mujer .... woman
el/la niño(a) .... child
la novia .... girlfriend, fiancée
el novio .... boyfriend, fiancé
los recién casados .... newly-weds
el soltero .... single man
la soltera .... single woman
el vecino .... neighbour
la viuda .... widow
el viudo .... widower

Adjetivos   **Adjectives**
adoptivo(a) .... adopted
casado(a) .... married
divorciado(a) .... divorced
familiar .... of the family
mayor .... elder
menor .... younger, youngest
quedar huérfano(a) ...... orphaned
separado(a) .... separated
soltero(a) .... single
último(a) .... last
viejo(a) .... aged, elderly, old
viudo(a) .... widowed

agnóstico(a) .... of no religion
anglicano(a) .... anglican
ateo(a) .... atheist
católico(a) .... Catholic
cristiano(a) .... Christian
hindú .... Hindu
judío(a) .... Jewish
musulmán(ana) .... Muslim
protestante .... Protestant
sij .... Sikh

El aspecto   **Appearance**
la alianza .... wedding ring
la barba .... beard
el bigote .... moustache
la cola de caballo .... ponytail
el flequillo .... fringe
las gafas .... spectacles
el peso .... weight
el tamaño .... size
la tez .... complexion
la trenza .... plait

For parts of the body see page 19

Adjetivos   **Adjectives**
blanco(a) .... white
bonito(a) .... pretty
bronceado(a) .... tanned
corto(a) .... short
de tamaño mediano ...... of average height
ensortijado(a) .... curly (frizzy)
feo(a) .... ugly
fuerte .... strong
gordo(a) .... big, fat
grande .... big, tall
guapo(a) .... handsome, beautiful
joven .... young
largo(a) .... long
negro(a) .... black
rechoncho(a) .... stocky, sturdy
rizado(a) .... curly (wavy)
rubio(a) .... blonde

delgado(a) .... thin, slim
lacio .... straight (hair)
pálido(a) .... pale
pelirrojo(a) .... red (hair)
pequeño(a) .... small
viejo(a) .... old

Mido...   **I am ... tall**
Mido 1 metro 45 .... I am 4ft 9in
Mido 1 metro 52 .... I am 5 ft
Mido 1 metro 60 .... I am 5ft 3in
Mido 1 metro 68 .... I am 5ft 6in
Mido 1 metro 75 .... I am 5ft 9in
Mido 1 metro 83 .... I am 6ft

Peso...   **I weigh...**
Peso 38 kilos .... I weigh 6 stone
Peso 45 kilos .... I weigh 7 stone
Peso 51 kilos .... I weigh 8 stone
Peso 57 kilos .... I weigh 9 stone
Peso 64 kilos .... I weigh 10 stone
Peso 70 kilos .... I weigh 11 stone

Los colores   **Colours**
amarillo .... yellow
azul .... blue
azul claro .... light blue
azul marino .... navy blue
azul oscuro .... dark blue
blanco .... white
castaño .... light brown, chestnut
(color de) malva .... mauve
gris .... grey
grisáceo .... greying
marrón .... brown
morado .... crimson, purple
naranja .... orange
negro .... black
rosa .... pink
verde .... green

El carácter   **Character**
la amabilidad .... gentleness
la amistad .... friendship
el amor .... love
la arrogancia .... arrogance
la benevolencia .... kindness
la bondad .... kindness
los celos .... jealousy
el chiste .... joke
la confianza .... confidence
el egoísmo .... selfishness
el encanto .... charm
la esperanza .... hope
la generosidad .... generosity
la imaginación .... imagination
la inquietud .... care, worry
la inteligencia .... intelligence
el orgullo .... pride
la pereza .... laziness
el sentido de humor ... sense of humour
el sentimiento .... feeling

Adjetivos   **Adjectives**
activo(a) .... active
agradable .... pleasant
alegre .... happy, cheerful
amable .... friendly, kind
atlético(a) .... athletic
callado .... quiet
contento .... pleased, happy
cortés .... polite
deportista .... sporty, athletic
divertido(a) .... amusing
enfadado(a) .... angry
enojado(a) .... angry, furious
estupendo(a) .... great
feliz .... happy
furioso(a) .... angry
gracioso(a) .... funny
importante .... important
infeliz .... unhappy, unfortunate
inteligente .... intelligent

pobre .... poor
serio(a) .... serious
simpático(a) .... nice
tímido(a) .... shy
tranquilo(a) .... calm
travieso(a) .... naughty; nasty

celoso(a) .... jealous
desagradable .... unpleasant
descortés .... impolite
encantador(a) .... charming
extraño(a) .... strange
hábil .... clever, skilful
honesto(a) .... honest
inquieto(a) .... anxious
listo(a) .... clever
loco(a) .... mad
mimado(a) .... spoiled
nervioso(a) .... nervous
orgulloso(a) .... proud
perezoso(a) .... idle, lazy
raro(a) .... odd
tonto(a) .... stupid
trabajador(a) .... hard-working
triste .... sad

ahorrador(a) .... careful with money
asqueroso(a) .... disgusting
astuto(a) .... wily, cunning
asustado(a) .... frightened
atolondrado(a) .... scatter-brained
bien educado(a) .... well-behaved
decepcionado(a) .... disappointed
deprimido(a) .... depressed
despistado(a) .... absent-minded
egoísta .... selfish
enamorado(a) (de) .... in love (with)
frugal .... thrifty, careful with
                                    money
habilidoso(a) .... gifted
hosco(a) .... sullen
insoportable .... unbearable
mono(a) .... cute

terco(a) .... obstinate
torpe .... clumsy

La nacionalidad   Nationality

antillano(a) .... West Indian
escocés(esa) .... Scottish
europeo(a) .... European
galés(esa) .... Welsh
indio(a) .... Indian
inglés(esa) .... English
irlandés(esa) .... Irish
paquistaní .... Pakistani

For other nationalities see page 88

Los animales domésticos   Pets

el animal .... animal
el caballo................... horse
el cachorro .... puppy
la cobaya .... guinea pig
el conejillo de Indias . guinea pig
el conejo................... rabbit
el gatito .... kitten
el gato .... cat
el hámster................. hamster
el loro....................... parrot
el pájaro .... bird
el periquito............... budgerigar
el perrito................... puppy
el perro..................... dog
el pez de colores .... goldfish
el ratón..................... mouse
la tortuga.................. tortoise

¿Cómo es?   What it it like?

grande .... big
joven .... young
juguetón(ona) .... playful (puppy, kitten)
obediente.................... obedient
pequeño(a) .... small
asustadizo(a) .... skittish (horse)
viejo(a)....................... old

For colours see page 28

Verbos útiles	Useful verbs
agradecer	to thank
aparecer	to appear
besar	to kiss
casarse con	to marry
charlar	to chatter
deletrear	to spell
describir	to describe
encontrar (ue)	to find
escribir	to write
estar	to be
estar de buen humor	to be in a good mood
estar de mal humor	to be in a bad mood
estar promitido(a)	engaged
firmar	to sign
gustar	to like, love
llamar	to call
llamarse	to be called
llegar a conocer	to get to know
llevar	to wear
nacer	to be born
nombrar	to name
parecer	to seem
parecerse a	to look like
pesar	to weigh
reconocer	to recognise
ser	to be
tener miedo	to be afraid
tener quince/dieciséis años	to be 15, 16 years old
vivir (en)	to live (at)

For festivals and celebrations see page 43
For jobs see page 70
For pocket money see page 37
For Saturday jobs see page 31
For hobbies and interests see page 31

Algunas frases

Me llamo David. Tengo dieciséis años. Vivo en Londres
My name is David. I am 16. I live in London

Mi cumpleaños es el diecinueve de mayo *My birthday is May 19th*

Nací en mil novecientos ochenta y dos *I was born in 1982*

Soy de Edimburgo *I come from Edinburgh*

Nací en York *I was born in York*

Soy inglés(esa)/escocés(esa)/galés(esa)/irlandés(esa) *I am English/Scottish/Welsh/Irish*

Tengo el pelo negro y los ojos marrones *I have black hair and brown eyes*

Tiene una barba gris *He has a grey beard*

Tengo un hermano y dos hermanas *I have one brother and two sisters*

David es mayor que Sue *David is older then Sue*

Mi padre es constructor, mi madre es enfermera *My father is a builder, my mother is a nurse*

Mis padres están divorciados *My parents are divorced*

Me llevo bien con mi hermano *I get on well with my brother*

Mi hermana es muy deportista *My sister is very keen on sport*

Tengo un gato y un perro *I have a cat and a dog*

Mi perro es grande y marrón *My dog is big and brown*

EL TIEMPO LIBRE Y EL FIN DE SEMANA

Palabras generales General

el	abono	subscription, season ticket
el	ambiente	atmosphere
el	concurso	competition
la	diversión	entertainment
la	fiesta	party
el	fin de semana	weekend
el	pasatiempo	pastime
el	tiempo libre	free time
las	vacaciones	holidays

La gente   People

el	actor	actor
la	actriz	actress
el/la	adolescente	teenager
el/la	árbitro	referee
el	campeón	champion
la	campeona	champion
el/la	cantante	singer
el	equipo	team
la	estrella de cine	film star
los	jóvenes	youth, young people
el/la	jugador(a)	player
el/la	miembro(a)	member

Las actividades del sábado
Saturday activities

el/la	cajero(a)	till operator
el	club de tenis/fútbol	tennis/football club
el/la	dependiente(a)	sales assistant
la	estación de servicio	filling station
la	mañana	morning
el	mercado	market
el	supermercado	supermarket
la	tarde	afternoon, evening
el	trabajo	work

Verbos útiles   Useful verbs

ganar dinero	to earn money

limpiar	to clean
repartir	to deliver
trabajar	to work
vender	to sell

Ayudando en casa Helping at home

arreglar mi dormitorio	to tidy my room
barrer	to sweep
cortar el césped	to mow the lawn
cultivar	to garden
dar de comer al gato	to feed the cat
fregar los platos	to wash up
hacer de canguro	to baby sit
hacer la compra	to do the shopping
hacer las tareas domésticas	to do housework
hacer mi cama	to make my bed
lavar el coche	to clean the car
limpiar	to clean
llevar al perro de paseo	to walk the dog
planchar	to iron
poner la mesa	to set the table
quitar el polvo	to dust
quitar la mesa	to clear the table
trabajar en el jardín	to work in the garden

En casa   Staying at home
¿Qué haces?   What do you do?

el	ajedrez	chess
la	cámara de fotos	camera
el	carrete	film (photography)
las	cartas	cards
la	cocina	cooking
la	colección	collection
la	costura	sewing
los	crucigramas	crosswords
las	damas	draughts
el	dibujo	drawing
la	fotografía	photography
la	historia de ciencia-ficción	sci-fi story
la	historia policíaca	detective story

31

el	juego de mesa	board game
la	lectura	reading
la	máquina fotográfica	camera
la	música	music
la	novela	novel
la	pintura	painting
el	póster	poster
la	revista	magazine
el	sello	stamp

La informática   IT

la	base de datos	data-base
el	botón de disparo	fire button
el	byte	byte
el	catálogo	disk manager
el	CD ROM	CD ROM
el	chip	chip
el	disco duro	hard disk
el	disquete	disk
la	impresora	printer
el	juego de ordenador	computer game
el	lápiz óptico	light pen
los	mandos	joy-pad
el	menú	menu
el	monitor	monitor
la	música por ordenador .	computer music
el	ordenador	computer
la	palanca de control ..	joystick
la	pantalla	screen
el	procesador de textos ...	word processing
el	ratón	mouse
el	teclado	keyboard
la	unidad de disco	disk drive
la(s)	vida(s)	life/lives
el	videojuego	video game

cargar	to load
formatear	to format
imprimir	to print
abrir.............................	to open
guardar	to save
editar	to edit

La música   Music

la	batería	drum kit
la	canción	song
la	cinta	cassette
el	clarinete.................	clarinet
el	coro	choir
el	disco compacto	compact disc
el	éxito	hit
la	flauta	flute
la	flauta dulce...........	recorder
el	grupo.....................	group
la	guitarra	guitar
el	instrumento	instrument
la	orquesta	orchestra, band
el	piano	piano
los	teclados	keyboard
la	trompeta	trumpet
el	violín....................	violin
el	walkman®	personal stereo

¿Adónde vas?   Where do you go?

el	baile	ball, dance
la	bolera	bowling alley
el	campo de deportes .	sports ground
el	cine	cinema
el	circo	circus
el	club	club
el	club de jóvenes	youth club
el	concierto...............	concert
la	conferencia	lecture
la	discoteca...............	disco
el	estadio	stadium
la	excursión	outing
la	exposición	exhibition
la	fiesta.....................	party
la	galería	gallery
el	jardín zoológico.....	zoo
la	piscina..................	swimming pool
la	pista de patinaje.....	ice rink
el	polideportivo	sports centre
la	reunión	meeting
la	sala.......................	room, hall
la	sociedad	society

el teatro .... theatre
la visita con guía .... guided tour

Los deportes   Sport

Palabras generales   General
el campeón .... champion
el concurso .... competition
el empate .... draw
el equipo .... team
el gol .... goal
el jugador .... player
el partido .... match
el torneo .... tournament

¿Qué deporte te gusta?
                    Which sport do you like?
las artes marciales .... martial arts
el atletismo .... athletics
el baloncesto .... basketball, netball
el balonmano .... handball
el balonvolea .... volleyball
los bolos .... bowling
el boxeo .... boxing
el ciclismo .... cycling
el críquet .... cricket
los dardos .... darts
los deportes acuáticos .. water sports
los deportes de invierno .... winter sports
la equitación .... horse riding
el esquí .... ski-ing
el footing .... jogging
el fútbol .... football
la gimnasia .... gymnastics
el golf .... golf
el hockey .... hockey
el judo .... judo
la natación .... swimming
el patinaje .... ice-skating
el patinaje sobre ruedas ... roller-skating
la pesca .... fishing
el ping-pong .... table tennis
el rugby .... rugby
el salto de altura .... high jump

el salto de longitud .... long jump
el snooker .... snooker
el tenis .... tennis
la vela .... sailing
el vuelo sin motor ...... hang gliding
el windsurf .... sail boarding

El equipo de deporte   Sports equipment
el balón .... football
el bate de críquet .... cricket bat
la bicicleta de montaña ... mountain bike
la caña de pescar .... fishing rod
los esquís .... skis
la gorra de montar ..... riding hat
el palo de hockey .... hockey stick
la pelota .... ball (small)
la plancha de surf ...... surfboard
la plancha de vela ...... sailboard
el traje de baño .... swimsuit
las zapatillas .... trainers

¿Cómo era?   What was it like?
aburrido(a) .... boring
agradable .... pleasant, nice
apasionante .... exciting
bueno(a) .... good
deportista .... sporty, keen on sport
divertido(a) .... amusing, funny
estupendo(a) .... great, super
fantástico(a) .... marvellous
fatal .... awful
fenomenal .... super
gracioso(a) .... funny
horrible .... ugly, horrible
impresionante .... impressive
inútil .... useless
no malo(a) .... not bad
otro(a) .... other
prohibido(a) .... not allowed
ruidoso(a) .... noisy
tremendo(a) .... great, brilliant

33

Comprando billetes   Buying tickets

el adulto .... adult	
el asiento .... seat	
el billete .... ticket	
el campo .... ground, pitch	
la costa .... cost	
la entrada .... entrance (cost)	
el/la estudiante .... student	
el grupo .... group	
el/la niño(a) .... child	
el precio .... cost, price	
la rebaja para niños .... reduction for children	
la tarifa de estudiantes .... student rate	
la tarifa reducida .... reduced rate	

Las horas de apertura   Opening times

a la una .... at one o'clock
dentro de media hora ... in half an hour
dentro de una hora .... in an hour
los días de fiesta .... on bank holidays
por la mañana .... in the morning
por la tarde .... in the afternoon
por la tarde .... in the evening

abierto .... closed
cerrado .... open
desde .... from
hasta .... until

Ir a la ciudad   Going into town

a pie .... on foot
en autobús .... by bus
en bicicleta .... on a bicycle
en el metro .... on the tube,
                            underground
en taxi .... by taxi
en tranvía .... by tram
en tren .... by train
en coche .... by car

el billete de ida .... single ticket
el billete de ida y vuelta .... return ticket
la correspondencia .... connection

la estación .... station
la estación de autobús .... bus station
la estación de metro .... tube station
el horario .... timetable
las horas punta .... rush hour
la línea de autobús .... bus route
la máquina de billetes .... ticket machine
la oficina de información .. information office
la parada de autobús .... bus stop
la taquilla .... ticket office

Adjetivos   Adjectives

directo(a) .... direct, through
obligatorio(a) .... compulsory
primero(a) .... first
próximo(a) .... next
segundo(a) .... second
último(a) .... last
válido(a) .... valid

¿Cuándo?   When?

durante el fin de semana ..... during the weekend
en diez minutos .... in ten minutes
en media hora .... in half an hour
en tres cuartos de hora . in three quarters of an
                            hour
en un cuarto de hora .... in a quarter of an hour
en una hora .... in an hour
normalmente .... normally, usually
por mucho tiempo .... for a long time
todavía .... still

For days of the week see page 92

Verbos útiles   Useful verbs

abrir .... to open
bailar .... to dance
cerrar (ie) .... to close
coleccionar .... to collect
comprar .... to buy
costar (ue) .... to cost
curiosear (en las tiendas) .. to go window
                            shopping
dar un paseo .... to go for a walk

descansar .... to rest
durar............................ to last
empezar (ie)................. to begin
escuchar....................... to listen (to)
escuchar cintas............. to listen to cassettes
escuchar discos compactos.. to listen to CDs
estar............................ to be
gustar mucho............... to like a lot
ir.................................. to go
leer .... to read
nadar .... to swim
pagar .... to pay (for)
quedarse .... to stay
regresar........................ to come back, go back
salir .... to go out
salir de casa .... to leave the house
ser .... to be
terminar....................... to finish

encontrar (ue) .... to find
correr........................... to run
dar una caminata.......... to hike, go for a long
                                        walk
ganar .... to win
ir a la ciudad................ to go to town
ir a ver......................... to go and see
ir en bicicleta.............. to cycle
ir de tiendas .... to go round the shops
jugar a los bolos........... to play skittles
jugar a las cartas .... to play cards
jugar un partido de tenis
            .... to play a game of tennis
mirar........................... to watch
practicar un deporte ..... to do a sport
sacar fotos .... to take photos
volver.......................... to return, go back
reservar una plaza........ to book a seat

cantar en el coro .... to sing in the choir
convalidar................... to stamp, validate

defender (ie).............. to defend
dibujar........................ to draw
esquiar........................ to ski
estar situado .... to be (situated)
hacer bricolaje............. to do odd jobs, DIY
hacer cola.................... to queue
hacer equitación .... to go horse riding
hacer vela................... to go sailing
hacer patinaje .... to skate
hacer patinaje sobre ruedas....to roller-skate
hacer una película de... to make a film
hacer windsurf............. to windsurf
interesarse en.............. to be interested in
ir a pescar................... to go fishing
marcar un gol .... to score a goal
modelar....................... to make models
parar(se) .... to stop
perder (ie) .... to lose
picar el billete............. to date stamp ticket
pintar.......................... to paint
relajar(se) .... to relax
tocar el clarinete .... to play the clarinet
tocar el piano.............. to play the piano
tocar el violín .... to play the violin
tocar el violonchelo ..... to play the cello
tocar la batería............. to play the drums
tocar la flauta .... to play the flute
tocar la guitarra .... to play the guitar
visitar un castillo .... to look round a stately
                                        house/castle

ir a la mezquita............ to go to the mosque
ir a misa .... to go to mass
ir a la sinagoga .... to go to the synagogue

For seaside holidays see page 80
For winter sports see page 81
For outings see page 81
For special occasions and festivals see page 43

Algunas frases

Juego al fútbol *I play football*

Toco el violín *I play the violin*

Me gusta ir de pesca *I like going fishing*

Ganamos el partido de fútbol *We won the football match*

Me interesa la música *I am interested in music*

Odio las telenovelas *I hate soaps*

Mi lectura preferida es la de ciencia-ficción *My favourite kind of book is science fiction*

EL DINERO PERSONAL

Palabras generales General

el billete (de banco) ... bank note
el cambio .... change (larger coins)
la libra esterlina .... pound
la moneda .... coin
la moneda suelta .... change (small coins)

cada semana .... each week
al mes .... per month

caro(a) .... expensive
mucho(a) .... a lot
pobre .... poor, badly-off
rico(a) .... rich

El dinero para gastos personales Spending money

el billete..................... ticket
los cigarillos............... cigarette
la cinta....................... cassette
el disco compacto ...... CD
la revista.................... magazine
la ropa .... clothes
el videojuego............. video-game
el walkman® .... personal stereo

las zapatillas de deporte ... trainers
los zapatos .... shoes

Ahorrando dinero Saving money

la bicicleta de montaña ... mountain bike
el ordenador .... computer
el regalo .... present
las vacaciones .... holidays

Verbos útiles   Useful verbs
comprar....................... to buy
ahorrar........................ to save
buscar empleo .... to look for a job
costar (ue) .... to cost
estar en números rojos. to be in the red
estar sin blanca........... to be broke
faltar dinero................ to be short of money
gastar.......................... to spend
gastar demasiado .... to spend too much money
malgastar.................... to waste money
necesitar .... to need
pedir prestado (i) .... to borrow

For other money words see page 76

Algunas frases

Gano...pesetas por hora *I earn ... pesetas an hour*

Trabajo los sábados *I work on Saturdays*

Empiezo a las ocho y termino a las cinco *I start at eight and finish at five*

Estoy ahorrando para comprarme un ordenador *I am saving up to buy a computer*

Lo he gastado todo *I've spent everything*

Estoy sin blanca *I'm broke*

LAS RELACIONES HUMANAS Y LA VIDA SOCIAL

Saludando　　Exchanging greetings

¡Hola! .... Hi!
Adiós .... Goodbye
Buenas tardes .... Good afternoon
Buenas tardes .... Good evening
Buenos días .... Good morning
¿Dígame? .... Hello (phone)
Hasta luego .... See you later
Hasta mañana .... See you tomorrow
Hasta pronto .... See you soon

¿Qué tal? .... How are you?
Muy bien, gracias .... Very well, thank you
Regular .... So-so
Le presento a Juan .... May I introduce Juan?
Le presento a mi padre
........................May I introduce my father?
Encantado(a) .... Pleased to meet you
¡Bienvenido! .... Welcome! (to a male)
¡Bienvenida! .... Welcome! (to a female)

Pasa .... Come in
Siéntate .... Sit down
Por favor .... Please
Gracias .... Thank you
Perdón .... Excuse me

Palabras de relleno　Fillers

Sí, claro .... Yes, of course
Con mucho gusto .... With pleasure
Creo que no .... I don't think so
Creo que sí .... I think so
De acuerdo .... Agreed
Me es igual .... I don't mind
No importa .... It doesn't matter
¡Qué bien! .... That's nice!
¡Qué lástima! .... What a shame!
Quizás .... Perhaps
Supongo que sí .... I suppose so

Pidiendo perdón　Apologising

Lo siento .... I am sorry
No lo hice de propósito .... I didn't do it on
　　　　　　　　　　purpose
No pasa nada .... No harm done
No importa .... It doesn't matter
De nada .... Don't mention it
No te preocupes .... Don't worry
¡Pelillos a la mar! .... Let's forget it!

Felicitaciones　　Best wishes

¡(Buena) suerte! .... Good luck!
¡Feliz Cumpleaños! ..... Happy Birthday!
¡Feliz Navidad! .... Happy Christmas!
¡Felices Pascuas! .... Happy Easter!
¡Feliz Semana Santa!... Happy Easter!
¡Feliz Año Nuevo! ...... Happy New Year!
¡Que tenga(n) un buen día!....Have a nice day!

Opiniones　　Opinions

Depende .... That depends
Es aburrido(a) .... It's boring
Es asqueroso(a) .... It's disgusting
Es delicioso(a) .... It's delicious
Es fatal .... It's awful
Es horrible .... It's lousy
Es interesante .... It's interesting
Es magnífico(a) .... It's superb
Me gusta .... I like...
Me gusta mucho .... I love...
No aguanto .... I can't stand...
No me gusta .... I don't like...
Odio .... I hate...
Prefiero .... I prefer...

amable .... kind
difícil .... difficult
fatal .... awful
flojo(a) en .... poor at
fuerte en .... good at

inútil para .... useless at
simpático(a) .... nice

Preguntas   Questions

¿Cómo es? .... What is ... like?
¿Cómo? .... How?
¿Cuál(es)? .... Which?
¿Cuándo? .... When?
¿Cuántos(as)? .... How (many)...?
¿Podemos..? .... Can we...?
¿Por qué? .... Why?
¿Puedo..? .... May I...? Can I...?
¿Qué? .... What?
¿Quién(es)? .... Who?

Problemas de adolescente
Teenage problems

La gente   **People**
el/la adolescente .... teenager
la   amiga .... friend, mate
el   amigo .... friend, mate
el/la gamberro(a) .... hooligan
el/la imigrante............. immigrant
el/la ladrón(ona) .... thief
la   novia.................... girlfriend
el   novio .... boyfriend
los padres .... parents
los profesores .... teachers

Los problemas   **Problems**
el   abuso .... abuse
la   actitud................... attitude
el   aprendizaje .... apprenticeship
el   asalto .... attack, mugging
la   asignatura .... school subject
la   ausencia sin permiso .... truancy
el   color .... colour
el   consultorio sentimental ...... agony column
los deberes .... homework
el   desempleo..................... unemployment
las diferencias generacionales.. generation gap
el   divorcio .... divorce

la   droga .... drug
el   empleo................... job
los exámenes .... examinations
la   falta de dinero........ lack of money
la   falta de transporte.. lack of transport
la   formación .... training
los granos................... spots, zits
el   hogar .... home
la   intimidación .... bullying
la   mentira .... lie
la   moda .... fashion
la   música pop .... pop music
el   paro .... dole
la   presión de los padres........parental pressure
la   piel .... skin
el   racismo................. racism
la   ratería .... shop lifting
el   refugio.................. refuge
la   rutina diaria .... daily routine
el   SIDA.................... Aids
el   trabajo .... work
el   trabajo escolar .... school work
el   uniforme escolar.... school uniform
el   vandalismo .... vandalism
la   violencia............... violence

Adjetivos   **Adjectives**
alcohólico(a) .... alcoholic
bien informado(a)........ well-informed
aburrido(a) .... boring, bored
bien educado(a) .... well-behaved
desaventajado(a).......... disadvantaged
estresado(a) .... stressed out
habilidoso(a) .... gifted
inteligente .... intelligent
lejos de la ciudad........ a long way out of town
mal informado(a)......... ill-informed
mimado(a).................. spoiled
obligatorio(a) .... compulsory
obvio(a)..................... glaring, obvious
perezoso(a)................. lazy
vagabundo(a).............. homeless

Expresiones	**Expressions**
Me aburre	It bores me
Me cansa	It makes me tired
Me crispa los nervios	It gets on my nerves
Me fastidia	It irritates me
Me molesta	It annoys me

Verbos útiles	**Useful verbs**
aceptar	to accept
acostarse (ue) tarde	to go to bed late
acostarse (ue) temprano	to go to bed early
arreglar el dormitorio	to tidy one's room
ayudar en casa	to help in the house
comprender	to understand
criticar	to criticise
decir la verdad	to tell the truth
discutir	to fight, dispute
divertirse (ie)	to have fun
dudar	to doubt
encontrar ... difícil	to find ... difficult
escabullirse	to skive off school

expulsar	to expel, send away
fregar (ie) los platos	to do the washing up
ganar dinero	to earn money
hacerse	to become
hacer novillos	to truant
levantarse tarde	to get up late
llevarse bien con	to get on well with
mentir (ie)	to lie
ocultar la verdad	to hide the truth
olvidar(se)	to forget
perder (ie)	to lose
permitir	to allow
repasar	to revise
robar	to steal
ruborizarse	to blush
tener que	to have to

For leisure time and activities see page 31
For café and restaurant see page 23
For TV, radio, music etc. see page 16

Frases y preguntas

¿Te llevas bien con tus padres/tu madre/tu padre/tu hermano/tu hermana?
Do you get on well with your parents/mother/father/brother/sister?
¿Tienes problemas en el colegio? *Have you any problems at school?*
¿Te permiten salir con amigos durante la semana/el fin de semana?
Are you allowed to go out with your friends during the week/at weekends?
¿De qué se discute en tu casa? *What do you argue about at home?*
¿Qué te fastidia? *What annoys you?*
Lo que me fastidia es... *What annoys me is...*

¿VAMOS A SALIR?

¿Adónde vamos?
Where shall we go?

la	sala de fiestas	nightclub
la	cafetería	café
el	cine	cinema
la	discoteca	disco
la	fiesta	party
el	parque	park
el	partido	match
la	piscina	swimming pool
la	pista de patinaje	ice rink
el	polideportivo	sports centre
el	teatro	theatre
las	tiendas	shops

Aceptar — Accepting

bueno	good
claro	of course
con gusto	with pleasure
con mucho gusto	gladly
de acuerdo	OK, agreed
depende	it depends...
fenomenal	super
gracias	thank you
Me gustaría mucho	I'd love to
por cierto	certainly
sí	yes
vale	OK

Negar — Refusing

Es imposible, porque...	It's impossible, because
Lo siento, pero...	Sorry, but...
No puedo	I can't
No estoy libre	I'm not free
no	no
desafortunadamente	unfortunately

¿A qué hora nos encontramos?
When shall we meet?

a las siete y media	at 7.30
en el fin de semana	at the weekend
en dos horas	in two hours
esta tarde	this afternoon
esta tarde	this evening
la semana que viene	next week
mañana	tomorrow
pronto	soon

For other clock times see page 91
For days of the week see page 92

¿Dónde nos encontramos?
Where shall we meet?

la	cafetería	café
el	cine	cinema
la	estación	station
la	parada de autobús	bus stop
el	restaurante	restaurant

For town and buildings see page 45

a la derecha de	to the right of
a la izquierda de	to the left of
delante de	in front of
detrás de	behind
en	in
enfrente de	opposite

Verbos útiles — Useful verbs

aceptar	to accept
agradecer	to thank
bailar	to dance
costar (ue)	to cost
debemos	we must
decidir	to decide
encontrar (ue)	to meet
esperar	to wait for
fijar una cita	to arrange to meet

41

invitar.......................... to invite
ir a ver.......................... to go and see
ir con............................ to go with
llegar .... to arrive
negar (ie) .... to refuse
olvidarse...................... to forget
pensar (ie) .... to think
poder (ue)..................... to be able to, can
preguntar .... to ask
querer (ie).................... to want to
saber............................ to know
salir .... to go out
sentir (ie) .... to be sorry
sugerir (ie)................... to suggest
tener lugar .... to take place
venir............................ to come
ver.............................. to see

Las diversiones   Entertainment

el   cine........................ cinema
el   concierto............... concert
la   discoteca............... disco
la   fiesta..................... party
el   teatro .... theatre

Comprando entradas Buying tickets

el   adulto .... adult
el   asiento .... seat
el   balcón................... circle
el   billete .... ticket
las butacas.................. stalls
el   coste .... cost
la   entrada.................. entrance (cost)
el/la estudiante............ student
el   grupo .... group
el/la niño(a) .... child
el   precio .... cost, price

la   rebaja para niños.... reduction for children
la   tarifa de estudiante. student rate
la   tarifa reducida .... reduced rate

¿A qué hora empieza?
What time does it start?

el   día de fiesta .... bank holiday
la   hora...................... hour
las horas de apertura ... opening times
la   mañana.................. morning
la   tarde .... afternoon, evening
una hora .... an hour
a la una...................... at one o'clock

cerrado .... closed
abierto........................ open
desde.......................... from
hasta........................... until

Verbos útiles   Useful verbs

actuar .... to act
buscar......................... to look for
costar (ue) .... to cost
durar .... to last
empezar (ie) .... to start
entrar......................... to go into
gustar mucho.............. to love
llegar......................... to arrive
salir........................... to go out
terminar...................... to end
viajar......................... to travel
vivir .... to live

See page 91 for clock times
See page 90 for numbers
See page 92 for days of the week

LAS FIESTAS

Celebramos	We celebrate
el Año Nuevo	New Year
el año nuevo judío	Rosh Hashana
el armisticio	Remembrance
Chanukah	Chanukah
Id	Id
el cinco de noviembre	Guy Fawkes Night
el día de Año Nuevo	New Year's Day
el día de la Madre	Mother's Day
el día de Navidad	Christmas Day
el día de Pascua	Easter Day
el día de San Valentín	St Valentine's Day
el Día de Todos los Santos	All Saints (Nov 1st)
Divali	Divali
el martes de carnaval	Shrove Tuesday
los Reyes	Twelfth Night
la Nochebuena	Christmas Eve
la Nochevieja	New Year's Eve
la Pascua judía	Passover
el primero de mayo	May 1st
el Ramadán	Ramadan
el Sabbath	Sabbath
la Semana Santa	Easter week

el Bar Mitzvah	Bar Mitzvah
la boda	wedding
el casamiento por la iglesia	church wedding
el cumpleaños	birthday
el enlace	marriage
la luna de miel	honeymoon
el matrimonio civil	registry office wedding
el nacimiento	birth
la recepción	reception
el santo	name day

Palabras generales General

el árbol de navidad	Christmas tree
el baile	ball, dance

el desfile	procession
la fiesta	party
la fiesta de cumpleaños	birthday party
los fuegos artificiales	fireworks
las hierbas amargas	bitter herbs
la historia	story
los huevos de azúcar	sugar eggs
los huevos de Pascua	Easter eggs
el muguete	lily of the valley
la música	music
Papá Noel	Father Christmas
el pastel	cake
las peladillas	sugared almonds
el regalo	present
la tarjeta	card

la catedral	cathedral
la iglesia	church
la mezquita	mosque
la sinagoga	synagogue
gurdwara	gurdwara

La gente	People
el/la amigo(a)	friend
la familia	family
los padres	parents
los parientes	relatives

cristiano(a)	Christian
hindú	Hindu
judío(a)	Jew
musulmán	Muslim
musulmana	Muslim
sij	Sikh

¿Cómo era?	What was it like?
divertido(a)	good fun
familiar	of the family
contento(a)	happy
religioso(a)	religious
ruidoso(a)	noisy

Verbos útiles	Useful verbs
bailar	to dance
beber	to drink
cantar	to sing
celebrar	to celebrate
comer	to eat
comprar	to buy
dar	to give
dar regalos	to give presents
enviar	to send
escuchar música	to listen to music
invitar	to invite
ir	to go
ir a un restaurante	to go to a restaurant
llegar	to arrive
pasar	to happen
pasarlo bien	to have a good time
quedarse	to stay
recibir amigos	to have friends round
rezar	to pray
tener lugar (ie)	to take place
visitar amigos	to visit friends

For other family words see page 26
For food see pages 53, 23
For recipes see page 55
For clothes see page 56

Frases y preguntas

¿Dónde pasas el día de Navidad/Chanukah/Divali/Id? *Where do you spend Christmas/Chanukah/Divali/Id?*

¿Qué haces? *What do you do?*

¿Qué comes? *What do you eat?*

¿Recibes regalos? *Do you have presents?*

Doy a mi padre un disco compacto de regalo *I give my father a CD as a present*

LA CIUDAD Y EL CAMPO

Palabras generales	General	La geografía	Geography
las afueras	suburbs, outskirts	la aldea	village
la agricultura	agriculture	el arroyo	stream
los alrededores	the area around	el clima	climate
el barrio	district in large city	el desierto	desert
el espacio	space	la isla	island
la industria	industry	el lago	lake
el medio ambiente	environment	la montaña	mountain
el ruido	noise	el país	country
el silencio	silence	la presa	dam
la zona edificada	built-up area	la provincia	province

el   pueblo.................... town; village
la   región .... region
el   río.......................... river
la   sierra..................... mountain range
el   valle....................... valley

La gente   People

el/la automovilista .... motorist
el/la cartero(a) .... postman
el/la ciclista .... cyclist
el/la ciudadano(a) .... city-dweller
el/la comerciante.......... trader
el/la granjero(a) .... farmer
el   guardia civil............. policeman (national)
la   guardia civil............. policewoman (national)
los habitantes............... inhabitants
el   hombre de negocios ...... businessman
los hombres........................ men
la   mujer de negocios......... business woman
las mujeres.................. women
los niños...................... children
el   peatón.................... pedestrian
la   policía..................... policeman (local)
la   policía..................... policewoman (local)
el/la trabajador(a) agrícola.. farm worker
el/la vendedor(a).......... seller
el/la tendero(a) .... shopkeeper

En la ciudad   In town

Los edificios   Buildings
la   abadía.................... abbey
el   aeropuerto............. airport
la   agencia de viajes.... travel agency
el   albergue juvenil ..... youth hostel
el   ayuntamiento .... town hall; city council
el   banco.................... bank
la   biblioteca.............. library
el   bloque de pisos ...... block of flats
el   castillo.................. castle
la   catedral................. cathedral
el   centro comercial .... shopping centre
el   cine...................... cinema

la   clínica.................... clinic
el   club de jóvenes ...... youth club
la   comisaría.............. police station
la   escuela.................. primary school
la   estación .... station
la   estación de autobuses.... bus station
la   estación de servicio....... petrol station
el   estadio.......................... stadium
la   estafeta de correos .... post office
el   estanco.................. tobacco kiosk
la   fábrica.................. factory
el   hospital................. hospital
el   hotel .... hotel
la   iglesia................... church
el   instituto .... secondary school
el   mercado................ market
el   monasterio............ monastery
el   museo................... museum
la   oficina.................. office
la   oficina de turismo.. tourist office
el   parque .... park
la   piscina.................. swimming pool
la   pista de patinaje..... ice rink
el   teatro.................... theatre
la   tienda................... shop
la   torre..................... tower

Los puntos de referencia   Landmarks
la   acera.................... pavement
la   aldea.................... village
el   aparcamiento .... car park
la   autopista............... motorway
la   avenida................. avenue
el   barrio................... suburb
el   barrio................... district, area
el   buzón................... letter box
la   cabina telefónica.... phone box
la   calle.................... street
el   camping................ campsite
la   carretera de circunvalación ..bypass
la   carretera radial....... ring road
el   centro de la ciudad........ town centre

45

el	cruce............................ crossroads
el	cruce para peatones....... pedestrian crossing
la	esquina .... corner
el	estanco................... tobacco shop, kiosk
el	final de la calle ...... end of the road
la	iglesia protestante .. Protestant church
el	indicador................ road sign, board
el	metro .... underground
la	mezquita................ mosque
el	monumento............ monument
el	palacio................... palace
la	parada de autobuses ...... bus stop
el	parque................... park
el	paseo .... wide street (with trees)
el	paso a nivel............ level crossing
el	paso subterráneo .... subway
la	plaza...................... place, square
el	polideportivo .... sports centre
el	pueblo................... town; village
el	puente................... bridge
el	puerto .... port
el	quiosco .... newspaper stand
la	rotonda .... roundabout
los	semáforos .... (traffic) lights
la	sinagoga .... synagogue
el	templo .... temple
la	terraza................... terrace (on pavement)
el	tráfico .... traffic
la	zona peatonal .... pedestrian precinct

En el parque   In the park

el	árbol .... tree
el	banco.................... bench
el	columpio............... swing
la	flor .... flower
la	fuente .... fountain
la	hierba .... grass
el	macizo.................. flower bed

En el campo   In the country

| la | aldea..................... village |
| el | árbol..................... tree |

el	bosque.................. wood
el	campo................... countryside, field
la	casa de vacaciones... second/holiday home
la	casita de campo ..... holiday cottage
la	colina .... hill
la	flor .... flower
la	granja .... farm
la	hierba .... grass
el	huerto................... orchard
la	naturaleza.............. nature
la	orilla..................... edge, bank
el	río......................... river
la	selva .... forest
el	sendero................. footpath
el	seto....................... hedge
el	tractor.................. tractor

En la granja   On the farm

la	charca................... pond
el	corral.................... farmyard
el	cortijo................... farmhouse
la	cuadra................... stable
el	espantapájaros .... scarecrow
el	granero .... barn
la	granja .... farm
el/la	granjero(a) .... farmer
el	heno .... hay
el	molino de viento.... windmill
el	nido .... nest
la	paja .... straw
los	productos agrícolas....... farm produce
el	remolque .... trailer
la	vendimia............... grape harvest
el/la	vinicultor(a)........ wine grower
la	viña .... vineyard

For animals see page 81

¿Cómo es?   What is it like?

| aburrido(a) .... boring |
| agradable.................... pleasant |
| ancho(a) .... wide |
| animado(a) .... lively |

46

antiguo(a) .... old, ex-
bonito(a) .... pretty, beautiful
bueno(a) .... good
cerca .... near
cercano(a) .... nearby, neighbouring
contaminado(a) .... polluted
encantador(a) .... charming
feo(a) .... ugly
grande .... big
hermoso(a) .... beautiful
histórico(a) .... historic
importante .... important
industrial .... industrial
interesante .... interesting
limpio(a) .... clean
moderno(a) .... modern
mucho(a) .... a lot of, many
natural .... natural
peligroso(a) .... dangerous
pequeño(a) .... small
pintoresco(a) .... picturesque
sucio(a) .... dirty
tranquilo(a) .... quiet, peaceful
triste .... sad
varios(as) .... several
viejo(a) .... old

¿Dónde está?   **Where is it?**
a .... at
a 10 kilómetros de .... 10 km from
a la derecha (de) .... on the right (of)
a la izquierda (de) .... on the left (of)
a lo largo de .... along
al lado de .... next to
allí .... over there
alrededor de .... around

cerca de .... near
cerca de aquí .... near here
contra .... against
debajo de .... under
delante de .... in front of
detrás de .... behind
en .... on
en el campo .... in the country(side)
en el pueblo .... in town; in the village
en (el) medio de .... in the middle of
enfrente de .... opposite
entre .... between
lejos de .... a long way from
muy cerca (de) .... very near (to)
situado(a) a .... situated (at)
todo recto .... straight on

For a list of countries see page 88

Verbos útiles   **Useful verbs**
cruzar .... to cross
estar .... to be
estar situado(a) .... to be situated
pasar .... to go past
perdonar .... to excuse
seguir (i) .... to carry on
seguir hasta .... to go as far as
ser .... to be
tomar .... to take
torcer (ue) .... to turn
ver .... to see
visitar .... to visit

For weather see page 48
For shops see page 52
For holiday words see page 77

Algunas frases

Vivo en Malvern desde hace diez años *I have lived in Malvern for ten years*

Malvern es un pequeño pueblo cerca de Worcester *Malvern is a little town near Worcester*

¿Qué hay que ver en Malvern? *What is there to see in Malvern?*

Hay las colinas, un museo pequeño y un parque *There are the hills, the little museum and a park*

Se puede ir al teatro, al cine o a la piscina *You can go to the theatre, the cinema or the swimming pool*

Se puede ir de caminata en las colinas *You can go for walks on the hills*

¿QUÉ TIEMPO HACE?

Palabras generales General

la	foto de satélite	satellite picture
el	pronóstico	weather forecast
el	pronóstico naviero .	shipping forecast
el	chubasco	shower, downpour
el	cielo	sky
el	grado	degree
la	lluvia	rain
la	niebla....................	fog
la	nieve.....................	snow
la	nube......................	cloud
el	sol.........................	sun
la	temperatura...........	temperature
la	tempestad..............	storm
el	trueno	thunder
el	viento	wind
el	arco-iris	rainbow
el	calor	heat
el	cielo cubierto	overcast sky
el	cielo despejado	bright period
el	claro	bright period
el	clima.....................	climate
la	estrella..................	star
el	granizo..................	hail
el	hielo	ice

la	humedad................	dampness, humidity
la	luna	moon
el	mar.......................	sea
la	marea	tide
el	mejoramiento	improvement
la	neblina..................	mist
la	precipitación.........	precipitation
la	presión..................	pressure
la	puesta del sol	sunset
el	relámpago.............	flash of lightning
la	salida del sol..........	sunrise
la	sombra..................	shadow, shade
la	visibilidad.............	visibility

Las estaciones   Seasons

el	invierno................	winter
el	otoño	autumn
la	primavera	spring
el	verano	summer
el	año	year
la	estación	season
la	mañana..................	morning
el	mes.......................	month
la	noche....................	night
la	tarde	afternoon, evening

¿Qué tiempo hace hoy?
What is the weather like today?

Está helando .... It is freezing
Está lloviendo .... It is raining
Está nevando .... It is snowing
Está nublado .... It is cloudy
Hace buen tiempo .... It is fine
Hace calor .... It is hot
Hace frío .... It is cold
Hace mal tiempo .... The weather is bad
Hace sol .... It is sunny
Hace treinta grados ...... It is 30 degrees
Hace viento .... It is windy
Hay niebla .... It is foggy
Hay tormenta .... It is stormy
Se hace de día .... It is light
Se hace de noche .... It is dark

¿Mañana...?   Tomorrow...?

Según el pronóstico
According to the weather forecast
Alcanzará 30 grados .... It will reach 30 degrees
Estará nublado .... It will be cloudy
Habrá claros .... There will be bright
                            spells
Habrá niebla .... It will be foggy
Habrá tormenta .... It will be stormy
Hará buen tiempo .... It will be fine
Hará calor .... It will be hot
Hará frío .... It will be cold
Hará sol .... It will be sunny
Hará viento .... It will be windy

¿Ayer...   Yesterday...

Estuvo helando .... It was freezing
Estuvo lloviendo .... It was raining
Estuvo nevando .... It was snowing
Estuvo nublado .... It was cloudy
Hizo 30 grados .... It was 30 degrees
Hizo buen tiempo .... It was fine
Hizo calor .... It was hot
Hizo frío .... It was cold

Hizo mal tiempo .... The weather was bad
Hizo sol .... It was sunny
Hizo viento .... It was windy
Hubo niebla .... It was foggy

... ¿o cuándo?   ...or when?

a menudo .... often
a veces .... sometimes
de vez en cuando .... from time to time
mañana .... tomorrow
normalmente .... usually
pasado mañana .... the day after tomorrow
(un) poco antes .... recently
(un) poco después .... shortly after

Adjetivos   Adjectives
agradable .... pleasant
azul .... blue
brumoso(a) .... misty
bueno(a) .... fine
caliente .... hot
cubierto .... overcast
de nieve .... snowy
despejado(a) .... clear
feo(a) .... awful
frío(a) .... cold
fuerte .... strong
ligero(a) .... light
lluvioso(a) .... wet
mal .... bad
mejor .... better
moderado(a) .... moderate
nuboso(a) .... cloudy
próximo(a) .... next
raro(a) .... rare
seco(a) .... dry
sofocante .... heavy, sultry
soleado(a) .... sunny
templado(a) .... mild
tormentoso(a) .... stormy
triste .... gloomy, dull
variable .... variable

Verbos útiles	Useful verbs
brillar	to shine
cambiar	to change
derretir (i)	to melt
desencadenarse	to burst
hacer buen tiempo	to be fine
helar (ie)	to freeze

llover (ue)	to rain
nevar (ie)	to snow
ponerse frío(a)	to get colder
ponerse templado(a)	to become mild
pronosticar	to forecast
soplar	to blow
tronar (ue)	to thunder

PREGUNTANDO EL CAMINO

¿Por dónde se va a...?
How do I get to...?

Perdóneme, señor	Excuse me (to a man)
Perdóneme, señora	Excuse me (to a woman)
¿Dónde está?	Where is...?
Muchas gracias	Thank you very much

Siga todo recto	Go straight on
Baje la calle	Go down the street
Tome el E4	Take the E4
Suba la calle	Go up the street

Tome la primera calle a la derecha	Take the first on the right
Tuerza a la derecha	Turn right
Tuerza a la izquierda	Turn left
Cruce el camino	Cross the road

¿Dónde está?   Where is it?

al lado de Correos	next to the post office
antes de llegar al quiosco	before you get to the kiosk
cerca	close by
cerca de aquí	near here
cerca de la plaza	near the square
delante del cine	outside the cinema
después del cruce	after the crossroads
detrás del teatro	behind the theatre

en la esquina de la calle	on the corner of the street
enfrente del banco	opposite the bank
entre el puente y los semáforos	between the bridge and the lights
lejos de la estación	a long way from the station

For landmarks see page 45

Las señales   Signs

circulen por la izquierda	keep to the right
desvío	diversion
no pisar la hierba	keep off the grass
obras en la carretera	work in progress, roadworks
peaje	toll
peatones	pedestrians only
prohibido el aparcamiento	no parking
prohibido el paso	no entry
prohibido ir en bicicleta	no cyclists
sentido único	one way

El mapa   The map

la autopista	motorway
la carretera principal	main road
la carretera secundaria	secondary road
la ruta de vacaciones	holiday route (HR)

Verbos útiles Useful verbs

andar .... to walk
bajar .... to go down
conducir .... to drive
conocer .... to know (place)
cruzar .... to cross
estar de pie .... to be on foot
ir.................................. to go
ir hasta........................ to go as far as...
marchar .... to go (of a vehicle)
saber .... to know (fact, how to)

seguir (i)..................... to continue
subir .... to go up
tomar........................... to take (a route)
torcer (ue) .... to turn
ver............................... to see

For town words see page 45
For shops see page 52
For address words see page 10
For car and public transport words see page 63

Algunas frases

¿Por dónde se va a la estación, por favor? *What is the way to the station, please?*

¿Dónde está la estación de autobuses? *Where is the bus station?*

¿Está lejos? *Is it far?*

¿A qué distancia está? *How far is it?*

Está a diez minutos a pie *It's a ten minute walk*

Está a cinco kilómetros *It's five kilometres*

¿Se puede ir en autobús? *Can we get there by bus?*

¿Tengo que tomar un taxi? *Do I have to take a taxi?*

HACIENDO COMPRAS

Palabras generales General

las afueras .... outskirts, suburbs
el centro comercial .... shopping centre
el centro de la ciudad . town centre
la tienda .... shop

La gente   People

el/la cajero(a) .... cashier
el/la cliente(a) .... customer
el/la comerciante .... (market) trader
el/la dependiente(a) ..... sales assistant
el/la gerente .... manager
el/la transeúnte .... passer-by

Las tiendas   The shops

el almacén .... department store
el autoservicio .... self service
el hipermercado .... hypermarket
el quiosco .... news stand, kiosk
el supermercado......... supermarket

el banco .... bank
la caja de ahorros .... savings bank
la estafata de correos . Post Office

la agencia de viajes.... travel agency
el boutique................ small shop
la carnicería............... butcher's shop
la charcutería............. pork butcher's,
                                       delicatessen
la confitería .... sweet shop
el estanco.................. tobacconist's shop
la farmacia................ chemist's shop
la ferretería............... hardware shop
el/la fotógrafo(a).......... photographer's
el/la frutero(a) .... fruit seller
la joyería .... jeweller's shop
la lechería................. dairy produce shop
la librería.................. bookshop
la limpieza en seco .... dry-cleaning

el mercado................. market
el/la óptico(a) .... optician
la panadería............... baker's shop
la papelería................ stationer's shop
la pastelería.............. cake shop
la peluquería............. hairdresser's salon
la pescadería............. fish shop
la tienda de comestibles.. grocer's shop
la tienda de ropa........ clothes shop
la tienda de vino........ wine shop
la tintorería................ dry cleaner's
la verdulería .... greengrocer
la zapatería................ cobbler's

En la tienda   In the shop

los alimentos.............. groceries
el artículo.................. article
el ascensor................ lift
la calidad.................. quality
el carrito................... trolley
la cesta .... basket
la entrada principal.... main entrance
la escalera mecánica .. escalator
el escaparate.............. shop window
el estante .... shelf
la etiqueta................. label
la exposición .... display
la marca .... make, brand
las mercancías............ goods, commodities
el mostrador .... counter
la planta alta.............. top floor
la planta baja .... ground floor
el precio .... price
el producto .... product
el recibo .... receipt
el sótano................... basement
el suelo..................... floor
el/la tendero(a) .... shopkeeper
el vestuario............... changing room

Señales, Letreros   Signs, Notices

abierto 7 días por semana.... open 7 days a week
autoservicio .... self-service
cerrado .... closed
cerrado por vacación.... annual holiday
de segunda mano .... second-hand
empujad...................... push
entrada........................ entrance
en venta aquí .... on sale here
horas de apertura .... opening hours
oferta especial.............. on special offer
paguen en la caja .... pay at the cash desk
por favor, no tocar .... please do not touch
precios fantásticos .... fantastic prices
rebajas........................ reductions; sales
saldo........................... sale
salida de urgencia .... (emergency) exit
se vende....................... for sale
tirad........................... pull

bastante .... enough
¿cuál(es)? .... which?
¿cuánto(a) (s)?............. how much/many?
demasiado(a) (s) .... too much, too many
desde .... from
mucho(a) (s) .... a lot of
por persona.................. per person
Quisiera....................... I would like
unos/unas.................... some
vale............................. that's fine

Comprando comida   Buying food

Las bebidas   **Drinks**
el alcohol.................. alcohol
el café....................... coffee
la coca cola®............. coca cola®
la leche..................... full milk
la leche desnatada ...... skimmed milk
la leche medio desnatada
.... semi-skimmed milk
la limonada................ lemonade
el té .... tea

el vino...................... wine
el zumo de fruta .... fruit juice

En la panadería   **At the baker's**
la barra de pan........... stick of bread
el bocadillo................ sandwich
el bollo...................... doughnut
el cruasán .... croissant
el pan .... bread
el pastel..................... cake
los pasteles................. pastries, cakes
la tarta...................... tart

En la tienda de comestibles   **At the grocer's**
el aceite.................... oil
el arroz..................... rice
el azúcar................... sugar
los cereales................. cornflakes
el chocolate .... chocolate
la crema.................... cream
el dulce..................... sweet
las especias .... spices
los fideos................... noodles
la galleta................... biscuit
la harina .... flour
el helado................... ice cream
el huevo.................... egg
la mantequilla............ butter
la margarina .... margarine
la mermelada............. marmalade, jam
la miel...................... honey
la mostaza .... mustard
la nata...................... cream
la pasta .... pasta
las patatas fritas .... chips; crisps
el pimiento .... pepper
el queso.................... cheese
el quiche................... cheese and egg flan
la sal........................ salt
la sopa...................... soup
el vinagre .... vinegar
el yogur.................... yoghurt

La carne	**Meat**
el	bistec .... steak
los	caracoles .... snails
la	carne asada .... joint, roast meat
la	carne de caballo ..... horsemeat
la	carne de vaca .... beef
la	carne de venado ..... venison
la	carne picada .... mince
el	cerdo..................... pork
el	chorizo.................. Spanish sausage
la	chuleta.................. chop, cutlet
el	conejo................... rabbit
el	cordero .... lamb, mutton
la	hamburguesa.......... hamburger
el	jamón serrano .... cured ham
el	jamón York............ ham
el	paté...................... pâté
el	pato .... duck
el	pavo...................... turkey
la	pierna de cordero ... leg of lamb
la	pollería .... poultry
el	pollo .... chicken
el	salchichón............. sausage
la	ternera .... veal

Las legumbres	**Vegetables**
la	cebolla.................. onion
el	champiñon............. mushroom
las	coles de Bruselas ... Brussels sprout
la	coliflor.................. cauliflower
los	guisantes............... peas
el	haba (f) .... broad bean
la	judía .... bean
la	judía verde............. green/French bean
la	lechuga .... lettuce, green salad
la	patata.................... potato
el	pepinillo .... gherkin
el	pepino................... cucumber
el	repollo .... cabbage
el	tomate................... tomato
la	zanahoria.............. carrot

el	ajo .... garlic
la	alcachofa .... artichoke
la	berenjena............... aubergine
el	brécol .... broccoli
el	calabacín .... courgette
la	espinaca................. spinach
el	maíz .... sweetcorn
el	pimiento rojo......... red pepper
el	pimiento verde....... green pepper
el	puerro................... leek
el	rábano .... radish
la	remolacha.............. beetroot

La fruta	**Fruit**
el	aguacate .... avocado
el	albaricoque............ apricot
la	avellana................. hazelnut
la	cereza .... cherry
la	ciruela .... plum
la	ciruela pasa........... prune
la	frambuesa.............. raspberry
la	fresa .... strawberry
la	grosella espinosa.... gooseberry
la	grosella roja........... red currant
el	kiwi...................... kiwi
la	lima...................... lime
el	limón.................... lemon
la	mandarina.............. tangerine
la	manzana .... apple
el	melocotón.............. peach
el	melón .... melon
la	nectarina............... nectarine
la	nuez...................... walnut, nut
la	naranja.................. orange
la	pera ....,..... pear
la	piña .... pineapple
el	plátano.................. banana
el	pomelo .... grapefruit
la	sandía .... watermelon
la	uva .... grape
la	zarzamora.............. blackberry

El pescado — Fish

el arenque	herring
el atún	tuna
el bacalao	cod
el cangrejo	crab
el (filete de) pescado empanado ...	fish fingers
el gamba	shrimp
la langosta	lobster
el lenguado	sole
los mariscos	sea food
los mejillones	mussels
la ostra	oysters
la raya	skate, ray
el salmón (ahumado) .	(smoked) salmon
la sardina	sardine
la trucha	trout

¿Cómo es? — What is it like?

amargo(a)	bitter
asado(a)	roast
asado(a) a la parilla	grilled (meat, fish)
bueno(a)	good
caliente	hot
casero(a)	home-made
delicioso(a)	delicious
dulce	sweet
excelente	excellent
fresco(a)	fresh, not frozen
frío(a)	cold
frito(a)	fried
hervido(a)	boiled
limpio(a)	clean
malo(a)	bad
medio hecho(a)	medium (meat)
medio~	half~
muy pasado(a)	well cooked
orgánico(a)	organic (vegetables)
poco hecho(a)	rare (meat)
muy poco hecho(a)	very rare (meat)
regional	local
relleno(a)	stuffed
salado(a)	savoury, salty
tostado(a)	toasted (bread)

Las recetas — Recipes

¿Cómo se hace eso? — **How do you make that?**

el ajo	garlic
la albahaca	basil
el azafrán	saffron
la canela	cinnamon
los cebollinos	chives
el cilantro	coriander
las especias	spices
el estragón	tarragon
el jengibre	ginger
la mejorana	marjoram
la nuez moscada	nutmeg
el perejil	parsley
la pimienta	pepper
el romero	rosemary
la sal	salt
la salvia	sage
el tomillo	thyme

al horno mediano	in a moderate oven
a temperatura baja	on a low heat
completamente	thoroughly
crudo(a)	raw, uncooked
guisado(a)	stewed
hervido(a)	boiled
picado(a)	minced
picante	spicy
rallado(a)	grated
rebozado(a) en harina ..	dipped in flour, floured
(bien) untado(a) con mantequilla	(well) buttered

aplanar	to roll
batir	to beat
calentar hasta que hierva ...	to bring to the boil
cocinar	to cook
condimentar	to flavour
cortar	to cut
cortar en pedazos	to cut up
cubrir	to cover
dorar	to brown, fry gently
escurrir	to drain

limpiar......................... to peel, clean
(re)llenar .... to fill
mezclar......................... to mix
necesita........................ you need, take
pelar .... to peel, clean
preparar .... to prepare
sazonar .... to season
verter........................... to pour

una cucharada.............. a tablespoonful
una cucharadita............ a teaspoonful
una pizca .... a pinch of

Pesos y medidas   Weights and measures
cien gramos de....... 100 grams of ...
la docena .... dozen
el gramo .... gram
el kilo .... kilo
la libra .... pound (lb)
el litro....................... litre
medio litro de .... half a litre of
la tonelada .... ton

el cuarto .... quarter
el medio .... half
el tercio .... third

la botella................... bottle
la canastilla.............. punnet
el jarro...................... jar, pot
la lata........................ box, tin
la loncha................... slice (cheese)
el paquete .... packet
el par........................ pair
el pedazo .... item, piece
la rebanada .... slice (bread)
el trozo .... piece
el tubo .... tube

Pagando   Paying
el billete de mil pesetas...1000 peseta note
la caja....................... cash desk
el cambio.................. change, currency

la cartera .... wallet
el código de barras .... barcode
el dinero.................... money
el dinero para gastos personales
.... pocket money
la libra esterlina......... £, pound sterling
la moneda.................. coin
el monedero .... purse
la peseta .... peseta
el precio .... price
el talonario (de cheques)... cheque book
la tarjeta (de crédito) .... (credit) card
la (tarjeta) Visa®....... Visa® card

Comprando ropa   Buying clothes
la moda .... fashion
el número .... size (shoes)
la talla .... size (clothes)

el abrigo.................... coat, overcoat
el bañador .... swimming trunks
la blusa...................... blouse
el calcetín.................. sock
los calzoncillos............ underpants
la camisa .... shirt
la camiseta .... T-shirt
el chandal.................. tracksuit
la chaqueta .... jacket
la corbata................... tie
la falda .... skirt
el jersey.................... pullover, jumper, sweater
los legins.................... leggings
las medias .... pair of tights
los pantalones .... pair of trousers
los pantalones cortos ... pair of shorts
el pijama .... pair of pyjamas
el sombrero .... hat
el sostén .... bra
los vaqueros................ pair of jeans
el vestido.................. dress
las zapatillas de deporte ... trainers
el zapato................... shoe

el anorak.................... anorak
la bata........................ dressing gown
el bikini .... bikini
la bota........................ boot
la bufanda.................. scarf
el camisón .... nightdress
el chaleco .... waistcoat
el guante.................... glove
el impermeable .... raincoat
la manopla................. mitten
el mono .... dungarees
la sandalia................. sandal
el traje .... (gent's) suit
el traje de baño .... swimsuit
el traje de chaqueta .... (woman's) suit
la zapatilla .... slipper

el anillo .... ring
el bolsillo.................. pocket
el bolso..................... bag
el botón .... button
la cinta...................... scrunchie
el cinturón .... belt
el collar .... necklace
la cremallera............. zip
el cuello.................... collar
la manga.................... sleeve
el pañuelo (de papel) ... (paper) handkerchief
el paraguas................ umbrella
el pendiente .... earring
el reloj...................... watch
la riñonera .... bumbag

Los materiales   **Material**
el algodón.................. cotton
el cuero..................... leather
la lana....................... wool
el metal..................... metal
el nailon.................... nylon
el oro .... gold
la piel .... leather
el plástico .... plastic

la plata .... silver
la seda .... silk

El maquillaje   **Make-up**
la barra de labios .... lipstick
el desmaquillador ...... make-up remover
la laca para las uñas... nail varnish
el perfume .... perfume
el rimel® .... mascara
la sombra de ojos....... eye shadow

¿Cómo es?   **What's it like?**
algo bonito .... something pretty
algo menos caro .... something less expensive
a rayas....................... striped
caro(a)...................... dear, expensive
claro(a)..................... light (colour)
corto(a) .... short
de segunda mano .... second hand
diferente.................... different
entero(a).................... whole, complete
estrecho(a)................. narrow, tight
fresco(a).................... cool, fresh
grande .... big
largo(a) .... long
libre.......................... free
ligero(a) .... light (weight)
nuevo(a) .... new
oscuro(a) .... dark (colour)
parecido(a) .... similar, the same
pequeño(a) .... small

¿Qué talla es?   **What size is it?**
Para mujeres   **For women**
el vestido.................. dress
el traje de chaqueta.... suit
el jersey.................... jumper

talla 34 .... size 8
talla 36 .... size 10
talla 38 .... size 12
talla 40 .... size 14
talla 42 .... size 16

grande .... large
pequeño(a).................... small
mediano(a) .... medium

Para hombres   **For men**
la chaqueta .... jacket
el traje .... suit

talla 46 .... size 36
talla 48 .... size 38
talla 50 .... size39-40
talla 52 .... size 42
talla 54 .... size 44

la camisa .... shirt

talla 36 .... size 14
talla 37 .... size 14½
talla 38 .... size 15
talla 39/40 .... size 15½
talla 41 .... size 16

¿Qué número calzas?
                    What size shoes do you take?
número 37 .... size 4
número 37½ .... size 4½
número 38 .... size 5
número 39 .... size 5½
número 39½ .... size 6
número 40 .... size 6½
número 40½ .... size 7
número 42 .... size 8
número 43 .... size 9
número 44½ .... size 10
número 45½ .... size 11
número 47 .... size 12

All European sizings given are approximate

¿Para quién es?   **Who is it for?**
Es para un regalo......... It's for a present
Es para mí .... It's for myself

Los problemas   **Problems**
el agujero.................. hole

la batería .... battery (torch etc.)
la fuga .... leak
las instrucciones para lavar
.... washing instructions
la inundación............. flood
la pila .... battery
el recibo .... receipt
la reclamación .... complaint

Adjetivos   **Adjectives**
demasiado ancho(a)..... too wide
demasiado caro(a) .... too dear
demasiado corto(a) ...... too short
demasiado estrecho(a) . too tight, too narrow
demasiado grande........ too big

amable........................ kind
atascado(a) .... jammed, stuck
decepcionado(a) .... disappointed
desgarrado(a) .... torn
encogido(a) .... shrunk
imposible .... impossible
limpio(a) .... clean
listo(a)........................ ready
lo siento mucho .... very sorry
malo(a)....................... bad
pinchado(a) .... punctured
posible........................ possible
práctico(a) .... practical
propio(a) .... own
roto(a) .... broken
sucio(a) .... dirty
sólido(a) .... strong, solid

¿Qué es lo que no funciona?
                    What is broken/not working?
el equipo de discos compactos....CD player
la lavadora................ washing machine
el lavaplatos .... dishwasher
la linterna eléctrica .... torch
la máquina fotográfica....camera
el ordenador .... computer
el reloj...................... watch

¿A quién llamo?   Who shall I ring?

El/la dueño(a) .... owner
el/la dueño(a) del garaje.... garage owner
el/la electricista............ electrician
el/la fontanero(a) .... plumber
el/la gerente .... manager
el/la mecánico(a) .... mechanic

Verbos útiles   Useful verbs

añadir .... to add
bastar........................... to be enough
comprar .... to buy
comprobar (ue) .... to check
costar (ue).................... to cost
dejar caer .... to drop
desear .... to want
devolver (ue) .... to take back
envolver (ue) .... to gift wrap, wrap up
escoger .... to choose
funcionar .... to work, function
odiar............................ to hate
preparar .... to prepare
prometer .... to promise
querer (ie).................... to wish, want
regresar........................ to come back
remendar (ie) .... to mend
reparar......................... to repair
romper......................... to break
tomar........................... to take
traer............................ to bring

aceptar......................... to accept
arreglar........................ to fix
contar (ue)................... to count
criticar........................ to criticise
dar............................... to offer, give (present)
deber .... to owe
desgarrar .... to tear, rip
dividir .... to divide
encogerse .... to shrink
fiarse de...................... to trust, entrust
garantizar .... to guarantee
guardar el recibo.......... to keep the receipt
gustar .... to please
hacer limpiar .... to have cleaned
hacer reparar .... to have mended
limpiar en seco .... to dry-clean
maquillarse................. to put on make-up
medir (i) .... to measure
obtener un reembolso .. to get one's money back
pedir prestado (i) .... to borrow
pesar........................... to weigh
preferir (ie)................. to prefer
probar (ue) .... to prove
reclamar .... to complain
sugerir (ie).................. to suggest
sumar .... to add up

Algunas frases

Dices:

¿Perdóneme, hay una farmacia cerca de aquí? *Excuse me, is there a chemist nearby?*

¿Venden...? *Do you sell...?*

¿Tiene azúcar, harina, aceite de oliva, huevos? *Have you any sugar, flour, olive oil, eggs?*

Preferiría... *I would prefer*

Me quedo con esto *I'll take this*

¿Cuánto es? *How much is it?*

¿Cuánto le debo? *How much do I owe you?*

¿Tengo que pagar en la caja? *Do I have to pay at the cash desk?*

No tengo moneda suelta *I have no change*

Sólo tengo un billete de mil pesetas *I've only got a 1000 peseta note*

¿Me puedo probar este jersey, por favor? *May I try on this jumper, please?*

Es demasiado grande/estrecho/pequeño *It's too big/too tight/too small*

¿Puedo pagar con tarjeta de crédito? *May I pay by credit card?*

¿Me lo envuelve, por favor? *Can you gift-wrap it for me, please?*

Es todo, gracias *That's all, thank you*

La dependiente dice:

¿Quién es el siguiente? *Who is next?*

¿En qué puedo servirle? *May I help you?*

¿Algo más? *Anything else?*

¿Tiene cambio? *Have you any change?*

¿Qué talla es Vd.? *What size are you? (clothes)*

¿Qué número calza? *What size do you take? (shoes)*

Algunos problemas:

Creo que hay un error *I think there has been a mistake*

Quiero cambiar esta falda *I would like to change this skirt*

He guardado el recibo *I have kept the receipt*

El color no me sienta bien *The colour does not suit me*

Perdóneme, estos calcetines no son del mismo tamaño *Excuse me, these socks are different sizes*

Seguí las instrucciones para lavar, pero este jersey (se) ha encogido *I followed the washing instructions, but this jumper has shrunk*

Este reloj ya no funciona *This watch doesn't go any more*

LOS SERVICIOS PÚBLICOS

En la estafeta de correos
At the post office

el buzón.................... letter box
la carta....................... letter
el/la cartero(a) .... postman, postwoman
el correo .... post, mail
el correo a recoger ..... post to be collected
la (estafeta de) correos....post office
el día .... day
la dirección............... address
el estanco.................. tobacconists
el giro postal.............. postal order
el impreso................. form
la moneda de cien pesetas
    .... a 100 peseta coin
el paquete .... parcel
el porte .... postage
la próxima recogida ... the next collection
la recogida................. postal collection
el sello....................... stamp
la semana.................. week
el sobre...................... envelope
la tarjeta postal .... postcard
la tarjeta telefónica de cincuenta unidades
    .... 50 unit phone card
la última recogida ...... the last collection
la ventanilla............... counter position

bien .... well
¿cuánto tiempo?........... how long?
¿cuánto? .... how much? how many?
el extranjero............... abroad
perdido(a) .... lost
por avión .... by air mail
por correo certificado .. by registered post
urgente .... urgent

En el banco   At the bank

el banco.................... bank
el billete de mil pesetas..... 1000 peseta note

la caja....................... till
el cajero automático .. cash machine
el cambio.................. change, currency
el cheque (de viajero) ....(travellers') cheque
la comisión................ commission
el dinero .... money
la documentación ...... proof of identity
el Eurocheque........... Eurocheque
la firma...................... signature
la libra esterlina......... £ sterling
el número de cuenta... account number
el pasaporte .... passport
la peseta .... peseta
el talonario de cheques ...cheque book
la tarjeta del banco .... bank card
la tarjeta de crédito.... credit card
el tipo de cambio .... exchange rate
la ventanilla de cambio...exchange office

por ciento .... per cent

Verbos útiles   Useful verbs

aceptar........................ to accept
cambiar .... to change
cobrar comisión.......... to charge commission
cobrar un cheque .... to cash a cheque
cobrar un giro postal.... to cash a postal order
contar (ue).................. to count
echar a correos .... to post
echar en el buzón........ to post
entrar.......................... to go into
enviar......................... to send
firmar......................... to sign
hacer seguir (i) .... to send on
hacer un error............. to make a mistake
ir .... to go
ir a la caja.................. to go to the cash desk
llamar por teléfono ...... to phone
rellenar el impreso....... to fill in the form
repartir el correo.......... to deliver the post
salir de .... to go out of

utilizar................. to use
valer........................ to be worth

Los objetos perdidos   Lost property

la bicicleta............... bicycle
el bolso.................... bag, handbag
la cartera.................. wallet
la llave.................... key
la maleta................... case
la máquina fotográfica....camera
la mochila.................. rucksack
el monedero................ purse
el paraguas................ umbrella
el talonario de cheques ...cheque book
la videocámara.......... video-camera

Hay ... dentro.............. There is .... in it

el color................... colour
el daño.................... damage
la descripción............ description
la documentación....... ID
la fecha................... date
la forma................... shape
el formulario............. form
la marca................... make

el pasaporte.............. passport
la recompensa........... reward
la satisfacción........... settlement
un tipo de.................. a sort of

Verbos útiles   **Useful verbs**
bajar........................... to go down
buscar........................: to look for
dejar........................... to leave
dejar caer.................... to drop
depositar.................... to put down
encontrar (ue)............. to find
informar..................... to report
ir .... to go
mostrar (ue)................ to show
ofrecer........................ to offer
olvidarse..,.................. to forget
perder (ie) .... to lose
poner........................... to put
rellenar....................... to fill in
robar .... to steal
viajar.......................... to travel

For telephone words see page 75
For money words see page 76
For other office words see page 72

Algunas frases

Quiero mandar este paquete a Gran Bretaña *I would like to send this parcel to Britain*

¿Cuánto cuesta mandar una carta a Gran Bretaña?
How much does it cost to send a letter to Britain?

Cinco sellos de cuarenta y cinco pesetas, por favor *Five stamps at 45 pesetas, please*

He perdido mi máquina fotográfica *I've lost my camera*

Lo dejé en el tren *I left it in the train*

Me han robado el monedero *I've had my purse stolen*

¿Hay que ir a la comisaría? *Do I have to go to the police station?*

No soy de aquí *I am not from this area, I'm a stranger here*

Estoy de vacaciones *I am on holiday*

LOS TRANSPORTES

Palabras generales General

la bienvenida .... welcome, reception
el día de fiesta .... public holiday
el extranjero .... abroad
la llegada .... arrival
la salida .... departure
las vacaciones .... annual holiday, leave
el viaje .... journey

Los medios de transporte
Means of transport

el aerodeslizador .... hovercraft
el autobús .... bus
el avión .... plane
la bicicleta .... bicycle
la bicicleta de montaña ... mountain bike
el cacharro .... banger (car)
el camión .... lorry
la camioneta .... van
el ciclomotor .... moped
el coche .... car
el coche de línea .... coach
el helicóptero .... helicopter
la hidroala .... hydrofoil
la hidroala a chorro .... jetfoil
el metro .... underground, metro
la moto(cicleta) .... motorbike
el transporte público .. public transport
el tranvía .... tram
el tren .... train

La gente   People

el/la automovilista .... motorist
el/la auxiliar de vuelo .. steward (plane)
el/la azafato(a) .... air steward(ess)
el/la ciclista .... cyclist
el/la conductor(a) .... driver
el/la conductor(a) de camiones
.... lorry driver

el/la conductor de camiones interurbanos
.... long-distance lorry driver
el/la dueño(a) de garaje ...... garage owner
el/la empleado(a) de la gasolinera
.... pump attendant
el/la mecánico(a) .... mechanic
el/la pasajero(a) .... passenger
el/la peatón(ona) .... pedestrian
el/la piloto(a) .... pilot
el policía .... policeman
la policía .... policewoman
el/la portero(a) .... porter
el/la revisor(a) (de billetes) .... ticket collector
el/la turista .... tourist
el/la viajero(a) .... traveller

Viajando en tren   Train travel

el andén .... platform
el AVE .... high speed train
el billete .... ticket
el billete de ida .... single ticket
el billete de ida y vuelta .. return ticket
el cambio de horario .. timetable change
el coche-cama .... sleeper, couchette
el coche-comedor ...... buffet (car)
la consigna .... left luggage (lockers)
la correpondencia ...... connections
el destino .... destination
el equipaje .... luggage
la estación de ferrocarril ... railway station
el ferrocarril .... railway
el (no) fumador .... (non-)smoker
el horario .... timetable
la información .... information
la llegada .... arrival
la parada de taxis .... taxi rank
la plaza reservada ...... reservation
la primera clase .... first class
el rápido .... express train
la recepción .... reception

el retraso................... delay
la sala de espera......... waiting room
la salida.................... departure
la segunda clase........ second class
el TALGO................. express
la taquilla................. ticket office
el tranvía.................. stopping train
el tren....................... train
el vagón.................... carriage
la vía........................ track

Viajando en autobús y en tranvía
Bus and tram travel

el altavoz................... loudspeaker
el billete.................... ticket
el bonobús................. book of 10 tickets
la estación de autobuses.... bus station
la línea...................... line, route
la máquina automática de billetes
.... ticket vending machine
la máquina de picar.... ticket validating machine
el número.................. number
la parada de autobuses...... bus stop
el precio (del viaje).... fare

con destino a................ going to
procedente de............. coming from

Cruzando el Canal de la Mancha
Crossing the Channel

el barco...................... boat
el mar........................ sea
el mareo..................... seasickness
el puerto.................... port
el puerto del ferry...... ferry terminal
el transbordador......... car ferry; shuttle
la travesía................. crossing
el túnel debajo del Canal de la Mancha
.... Channel Tunnel

encrespado.................. rough
puntual....................... on time
tarde.......................... late
tranquilo.................... smooth

Viajando en avión Flying

el aeropuerto............. airport
el aterrizaje................ landing
el avión..................... plane
la cabina.................... cabin
el cinturón de seguridad . seat belt
la clase turista........... tourist class
el despegue................ take off
el embarcamiento...... boarding
el jumbo.................... jumbo jet
la llamada................. call
la puerta.................... gate
la puntualidad........... punctuality
el retraso................... delay
la terminal................. air terminal
el vuelo..................... flight

Viajando en coche Going by car

la autopista................ motorway
la carretera nacional .. main road
la carretera secundaria...... secondary road
la red de autopistas.... motorway network
la ruta de vacación..... holiday route

el aceite..................... oil
el aparcamiento......... car park, parking
el área (f) de descanso...... picnic area
el atasco.................... traffic jam
la calzada.................. roadway
el camión................... HGV, lorry
la curva..................... bend
el desvío.................... diversion
la documentación...... ID
el embotellamiento.... traffic jam
la estación de servicio....... petrol station
el final...................... end
el garaje.................... garage
la hora punta............. rush hour
el humo..................... smoke
el número.................. number
las obras.................... roadworks
el peaje..................... toll

la retención	hold up, delay
los servicios	toilets
la velocidad	speed

la acera	pavement
la autoescuela	driving school
el carnet de conducir	driving licence
el carril de urgencia	emergency escape lane
el casco	helmet
el código de la circulación	highway code
el cruce	crossroads
las líneas divisorias	road markings
el mapa	map
la mediana	central reservation
el peligro	danger
la poliza de seguros	insurance policy
la preferencia	right of way
la prioridad	priority
la rotonda	roundabout
los semáforos	traffic lights
el seguro	insurance
las señales	road signs
el tráfico lento	slow moving traffic
el/la vigilante (de paso de peatones)	crossing patrol

Mi coche está averiado
My car has broken down

la avería	breakdown
la batería	battery
el depósito de gasolina	petrol tank
el faro	headlight
el freno	brake
la llave de coche	car key
la marca	make
el motor	engine
el neumático	tyre
el parabrisas	windscreen
el pinchazo	puncture
la puerta	door
el ruido	noise
el servicio de avería	breakdown service
el tubo de escape	exhaust pipe

el acelerador	accelerator
la aleta	wing
la caja de cambio	gearbox
el capó	bonnet
el catalizador	catalytic converter
el cinturón de seguridad	seat belt
el claxon	horn
el embrague	clutch
el intermitente	indicator light
el limpiaparabrisas	windscreen wipers
las luces traseras	rear lights
el maletero	boot
los parachoques	bumpers
la parte delantera	front
la parte trasera	back
la pieza de repuesto	spare part
el radiador	radiator
el asiento	seat
la cerradura	lock
el espejo retrovisor	rear view mirror
las marchas	gears
la rueda (de repuesto)	(spare) wheel
las velocidades	gears; speeds
la ventanilla	window
el volante	steering wheel

Verbos útiles   Useful verbs

averiarse	to break down
esperar	to wait for
funcionar	to work
llamar por teléfono	to phone
marchar	to work
parar en seco	to stop dead
pinchar	to burst (tyre)
reparar	to fix, repair
toser	to cough

En la estación de servicio
At the petrol station

el aceite	oil
el agua	water
el aire	air

el anticongelante........ anti-freeze
la bebida.................... drink
el carburante............. fuel
el/la empeado(a) de la gasolinera
.... pump attendant
el gas-oil.................... diesel
la gasolina .... petrol
la gasolina con plomo....... leaded petrol
la gasolina sin plomo........ unleaded petrol
la lata de aceite.......... can of oil
el litro......................... litre
el mapa...................... map
el nivel .... level
la presión de los neumáticos ..... tyre pressure
la super sin plomo ..... super unleaded

Un accidente   An accident

La gente   People
"agente" .... "officer"
el/la bombero(a) .... fireman
el/la ciclista .... cyclist
el/la conductor(a) de ambulancia
.... ambulance driver
el/la conductor(a) de coche...... car driver
el/la culpable .... the culprit
el/la enfermero(a) .... nurse
el/la médico(a)............. doctor
el/la motociclista .... motorcyclist
el/la peatón(ona).......... pedestrian
el policía.................... policeman
la policía.................... policewoman
el/la testigo(a).............. witness
el/la transeúnte .... passer-by

Palabras generales   General
el accidente de coche. car accident
el accidente múltiple.. pile-up
la ambulancia .... ambulance
la camilla................... stretcher
la caución .... bail bond
el choque.................. collision
el coche de línea .... coach
el código de la circulación ..... highway code

la comisaría............... police station
el consulado .... consulate
la culpa..................... fault
el daño .... damage
la declaración .... statement
la dirección............... direction
la disculpa .... excuse
el impacto .... impact
el peligro................... danger
el permiso .... permission
la policía .... police
los primeros auxilios ... first aid
la prioridad............... priority
el problema .... problem
la prueba del alcohol . breath test
el riesgo .... risk
las señas..................... address
el servicio de rescate . police rescue service
la unidad móvil de urgencia
.... mobile emergency unit
el vehículo................ vehicle

For weather words see page 48

¿Es grave?   Is it serious?
conmocionado(a)......... in shock
despacio .... slowly
grave .... serious
herido(a) .... injured
inconsciente .... unconscious
inquieto(a).................. anxious
muerto(a) .... dead
rápido(a) .... quickly
sorprendente............... surprising
urgente .... urgent

Exclamaciones   Exclamations
¡Ay de mí!.................. Alas!
¡Ay! .... Oh!
¡Cuidado!.................... Look out!
¡De acuerdo! .... OK, agreed!
¡Dios mío!.................. My goodness!
¡Fuego! .... Fire!

¡Lo siento!................... Sorry!
¡No te preocupes! .... Never mind!
¡Socorro! .... Help!
¡Tanto mejor! .... So much the better!

Verbos útiles   **Useful verbs**
adelantar...................... to overtake
adelantarse.................. to go forward
alquilar .... to hire
andar .... to walk, go on foot
aterrizar .... to land
buscar.......................... to look for
comprar .... to buy
conducir .... to drive, travel (by car)
consultar...................... to consult
dejar .... to get off
despegar .... to take off (plane)
inflar los neumáticos.... to pump up the tyres
ir.................................. to go
ir en autobús................ to go by bus
ir en bicicleta............... to go by bike
ir en coche de línea...... to go by coach
ir en tren...................... to go by train
lavar el parabrisas........ to wash the windscreen
(re)llenar con gasolina . to fill up with petrol
marchar .... to go (vehicle)
pasar............................ to pass (time)
picar .... to time stamp a ticket
subir a la cubierta .... to go up on deck
traer............................. to fetch
volar (ue)..................... to fly (person)

aparcar......................... to park
bajar .... to get off, to get out of
cambiar........................ to change

coger .... to catch the train/coach
comprobar (ue)............. to examine, check
controlar...................... to check
encontrar una plaza...... to find a seat
esperar......................... to wait (for)
llegar........................... to arrive
montar......................... to get on, to get into
perder (ie) .... to miss (train)
pilotar.......................... to fly (plane)
salir (de)...................... to leave (from)
utilizar......................... to use

arrancar....................... to start the engine
averiarse...................... to break down
cambiar de marcha ...... to change gear
chocar contra............... to collide with
cruzar .... to cross
dar marcha atrás .... to reverse
durar............................ to last
encender los faros........ to switch on the
                     headlights
estar situado(a) .... to be situated
frenar .... to brake
informarse (sobre) .... to find out (about)
parar el motor.............. to switch off the engine
parar(se) .... to stop
regresar .... to return home
salir .... to go out
saltarse un semáforo en rojo
                   to jump the lights
tocar el claxon............. to sound the horn
torcer........................... to turn
tropezar con................. to bump into
volcar .... to knock, turn over

Algunas frases

El tren sale del andén número ocho *The train leaves from platform 8*

El tren sale a las doce y media, a mediodía *The train leaves at 12.30, midday*

¿Hay que hacer transbordo? *Do I have to change?*

Quiero un billete de ida y vuelta de segunda clase, por favor *I would like a second class return, please*

¿Dónde puedo aparcar? *Where can I park?*

Treinta litros de gasolina sin plomo, por favor *30 litres of lead-free, please*

Mi coche está averiado *My car has broken down*

El motor no arranca *The engine will not start*

Voy a tomar el avión de Londres a Alicante *I'm flying from London to Alicante*

LA FORMACIÓN Y EL TRABAJO

Los exámenes y después
Exams and afterwards

Palabras generales   General

la   concentración......... concentration

el   examen.................. examination

el   examen escrito....... written test

el   examen oral.......... speaking test

los exámenes de prueba....mock exams

la   nota .... mark

la   nota de aprobado.... pass mark

la   pregunta................. question

la   respuesta............... answer

la   respuesta correcta .. right answer

la   respuesta equivocada ..wrong answer

el   trabajo .... work

La gente   People

el/la aprendiz(a).......... apprentice, trainee

el/la candidato(a) .... candidate

el/la estudiante............ student

el/la examinador(a)...... examiner

el/la profe(sor) (a) .... teacher

Adjetivos   Adjectives

aburrido(a) .... boring

como grupo .... as a group

difícil .... difficult

divertido(a) .... amusing, "fun"

individual .... individual

próximo(a) .... next

último(a) .... last

Verbos útiles   Useful verbs

aprobar (ue)............... to pass an exam

contestar la pregunta.... to answer the question

estudiar .... to study

examinarse .... to take an exam

preparar...................... to prepare for

repasar....................... to revise

suspender .... to fail an exam

trabajar...................... to work

Pasando a tercero de BUP
                    Going into the Sixth Form

el   bachillerato superior..... A level equivalent

el   bachillerato elemental... GCSE equivalent

las ciencias................. sciences

la   enseñanza .... teaching
los estudios científicos........ scientific studies
los estudios literarios ... literary studies
los idiomas .... languages
el   instituto técnico ..... technical school
el   nivel .... level

La educación superior
Higher education

la   academia de música ...... academy of music
el   colegio de la marina de guerra
     .... navy college
el   colegio del ejército........ army college
la   escuela de magisterio
     .... teacher training college
la   Facultad de Ciencias ..... faculty of Science
la   Facultad de Filosofía y Letras
     .... faculty of arts
la   Facultad de Medicina.... medical school
la   licenciatura .... degree
la   universidad .... university

La Formación   Training

el   aprendizaje .... apprenticeship
las clases nocturnas..... evening classes
la   competición .... competition
la   formación profesional... vocational training
el   plan de formación.. training scheme
el   plan de formación para jóvenes
     .... youth training scheme

Verbos útiles   Useful verbs

estudiar la licenciatura........ to read for a degree
hacer un curso de formación
     .... to go on a training course
obtener el título .... to graduate
recibir formación........ to receive training
tener buenas referencias
     .... to have good references

BUSCANDO UN EMPLEO

Palabras generales General

el carácter.................. character
el carnet de conducir.. driving licence
el comercio............... trade
el desempleo............. unemployment
el empleo................... situation, job
el equipo................... team
el negocio................. business
la personalidad......... personality
la profesión............... career
el puesto................... post, job
el salario................... salary
el sueldo................... pay, salary
la suma de dinero....... sum of money
el trabajo a tiempo completo
.... full-time work
el trabajo por horas.... part-time work
el trabajo temporal..... temporary work

Solicitando un empleo
Applying for a job

el apellido.................. surname
la carta...................... letter
el curriculum (vitae) .. CV, curriculum vitæ
la escritura................ handwriting
el estado (familiar) .... family status
la fecha de nacimiento....date of birth
la licenciatura............ ....degree
el lugar de nacimiento .... place of birth
el nombre.................. first name
la ortografía............... spelling
la profesión............... profession
las cualificaciones profesionales
.... professional qualifications

Verbos útiles   Useful verbs
acusar recibo de una carta
.... to acknowledge receipt of a letter
aconsejar .... to advise
dar............................. to give, hand out
hacer un curso .... to go on a course

trabajar....................... to work

La gente   People

el/la aprendiz(a) .... apprentice
el/la colega................. colleague
el/la director(a)........... director, manager
el/la director(a) de márketing
.... marketing director
el/la director(a) de ventas......sales manager
el/la director(a) de personal ...personnel director
el/la empleado(a)......... employee
las empresarios(as)...... businessmen, managers
la gerencia................. management
el/la gerente............... person in charge of
                          business, manager
el/la huelguista........... striker
el/la jefe(a) de ventas... sales manager
el/la jefe de personal.... personnel manager
el/la parado(a) .... unemployed person
el/la patrón(ona) .... boss, employer
el/la secretario(a)........ secretary
el/la sindicalista.......... trade unionist

Los empleos   Jobs

Las profesiones   Professions
el/la abogado(a).......... lawyer
el/la asistente(a) social. social worker
el/la contable............... accountant
el/la dentista............... dentist
el/la director(a)........... director
el/la director(a) de instituto .... headteacher
el/la diseñador(a)......... designer
el/la diseñador(a) de interiores
.... interior designer
el/la doctor(a)............. doctor
el/la enfermero(a) .... nurse
el/la funcionario(a)...... civil servant
el/la informático(a)...... computer scientist
el/la ingeniero(a) .... engineer
el/la maestro(a)........... primary teacher
el/la médico(a) .... doctor

70

el/la músico(a) .... musician
el/la periodista .... journalist
el/la político(a) .... politician
el/la profesor(a) .... teacher (secondary)
el/la programador(a) .... programmer
el/la veterinario(a) .... vet

Otras profesiones   Other professions
el/la arquitecto(a) .... architect
el/la asesor(a) .... consultant
la   azafata .... air hostess
el/la bibliotecario(a)..... librarian
el/la científico(a) .... scientist
el/la cirujano(a) .... surgeon
el/la escritor(a) .... writer
el/la fisioterapeuta .... physiotherapist
el/la investigador(a) ..... research worker
el/la meteorólogo(a)..... meteorologist
el/la químico(a) .... chemist (scientist)

En la calle   In the high street
el/la agente de viajes.... travel agent
el/la agente inmobiliario ...estate agent
el/la cajero(a).............. till operator, cashier
el/la carnicero(a).......... butcher
el/la comerciante.......... shopkeeper
el/la constructor(a)....... builder
el/la dependiente.......... sales assistant
el/la dueño(a) de garaje....... garage owner
el/la farmacéutico(a) .... chemist (pharmacist)
el/la florista .... florist
el/la fotógrafo(a).......... photographer
el/la frutero(a) .... fruitseller
el/la hotelero(a) .... hotelier
el/la intérprete............. interpreter
el/la panadero(a) .... baker
el/la peluquero(a)......... hairdresser
el/la pescadero(a) .... fishmonger
el/la tendero(a) .... shopkeeper
el/la vendedor(a) de periódicos
.... newsagent
el/la verdulero(a) .... greengrocer

Trabajadores cualificedos   Skilled workers
el/la artesano(a) .... craftsman(woman)
el/la carpintero(a) .... carpenter
el/la electricista .... electrician
el/la fontanero(a) .... plumber
el   hombre de negocios.... businessman
el/la jardinero(a) .... gardener
el/la mecánico(a) .... mechanic
el/la mecanógrafo(a).... typist
la   mujer de negocios....... businesswoman
el/la oficinista............. office worker
el/la organizador(a) ..... organiser; presenter
el/la pintor(a)............... painter
el/la secretario(a) .... secretary
el/la taquimecanógrafo(a) ......shorthand typist
el/la técnico(a)............. technician

Otras ocupaciones   Other occupations
el   ama de casa (f) ...... housewife
el/la árbitro(a) .... referee
el/la bombero(a) .... fireman(woman)
el   camarero............. waiter
el/la cantante .... singer
el/la cartero(a) .... postman(woman)
el/la cocinero(a)........... cook
el/la conductor(a) de ambulancia
.... ambulance driver
el/la conductor(a) de autobús... bus driver
el/la conductor(a) de camión ... lorry driver
el/la conductor(a) de taxi........ taxi driver
el/la dietético(a).......... dietician
el/la ejecutivo(a).......... executive
el/la granjero(a) .... farmer
el/la instructor(a) .... instructor
el/la jefe(a) .... chef; boss
el/la marinero(a) .... sailor
el/la minero(a) .... miner
el/la obrero(a)............. worker
el   pescador .... fisherman
la   pescadora............. fisherwoman
el/la piloto(a).............. pilot
el   policía .... policeman

la policía.................... policewoman
el/la portero................. caretaker
el/la salvavidas .... lifeguard
el/la soldado(a) .... soldier

El lugar de trabajo The workplace

el colegio................... school
la empresa .... firm
la fábrica .... factory
el hospital .... hospital
el laboratorio .... laboratory
la oficina .... office
la tienda.................... shop

al aire libre .... outdoors
dentro .... indoors

For list of shops see page 52
For list of places of education see page 1
For list of other buildings see page 45

En la oficina In the office

la agenda .... diary
la cita....................... appointment
el contestador automático
.... answering machine
el correo .... post, mail
el fax .... fax machine
el formulario............. form
la grapa..................... staple
la grapadora.............. stapler
la guía telefónica .... phone book
la hoja de papel.......... sheet of paper
el impreso................. form
la impresora.............. printer
el número de fax........ fax number
el número de teléfono .... phone number
el ordenador .... PC, computer
el retroproyector .... overhead projector
la reunión .... meeting
el sello...................... stamp
el sindicato .... union
el sobre..................... envelope

la tinta...................... ink

For other IT words see page 32

Letreros, Señales Notices, Signs

abierto........................ open
caballeros................... men's toilets
cerrado....................... closed
damas......................... women's toilets
empujad .... push
entrada .... entrance
peligro........................ danger
prohibido entrar........... no entry
prohibido fumar .... no smoking
puerta de la fábrica...... factory gate
recepción.................... reception
salida......................... way out, exit
salida de urgencia........ emergency exit
secretaria................... secretary
tirad........................... pull

Ventajas y desventajas Advantages and disadvantages

los trabajos no fijos..... jobs with no security
el trabajo en la cadena de montaje
.... assembly line work
las horas de trabajo ..... hours of work
el trabajo de adentro .. indoor work
el trabajo al aire libre. outdoor work
el trabajo sedentario .. a sitting down job

Verbos útiles Useful verbs

ayudar a la gente .... to help people
ampliar la experiencia . to broaden one's experience
estar aislado(a) .... to be isolated
hacer investigaciones... to do research
llevar uniforme........... to wear uniform
recibir propinas .... to get tips
teclear datos .... to key in data
trabajar a tiempo completo
.... to work full-time
trabajar al aire libre ..... to work outdoors

trabajar con cifras .... to work with figures
trabajar día y noche ..... to work day and night
trabajar los fines de semana
.... to work weekends
trabajar para la conservación
.... to work for conservation
trabajar para sí mismo.. to work for oneself
trabajar por horas......... to work part-time
trabajar por la tarde...... to work evenings
utilizar un ordenador.... to use a computer
utilizar un procesador de textos
.... to use a word processor
viajar alrededor del mundo
.... to travel round the world
volverse (ue) rico(a) .... to get rich

Las cualidades   Qualities

la buena salud............ good health
la cortesía .... politeness
la destreza................. dexterity
el discernimiento .... judgment
la inteligencia .... intelligence
la paciencia............... patience
el sentido artístico...... artistic sense
el sentido del humor .. sense of humour

con experiencia .... experienced
cortés........................... polite
honrado(a).................. honest
incansable................... not easily tired
inteligente .... intelligent
paciente....................... patient
trabajador(a)............... hard-working

Verbos útiles   Useful verbs
cooperar .... to cooperate
despedir (i) .... to lay off, make
                                         redundant
estar bien organizado(a)
.... to be well-organised
estar en paro................ to be unemployed
ganar........................... to earn
interesarse en la informática
.... to be interested in IT
ir bien vestido(a) .... to be well-dressed
jubilarse .... to retire
llegar a tiempo............. to arrive on time
llegar con retraso........ to be late
mandar un fax .... to fax, send a fax
ponerse en huelga........ to go on strike
respetar al cliente......... to have respect for the
                                         customer
trabajar....................... to work

Algunas frases
¿Qué vas a hacer el año que viene? *What are you going to do next year?*
Voy a dejar el colegio *I'm going to leave school*
Voy a trabajar como constructor con mi padre *I'm going to work as a builder with my father*
Voy a ser aprendiz(a) *I am going to do an apprenticeship*
Voy a estudiar idiomas modernos *I'm going to do modern languages*
Me gustaría estudiar en la universidad *I would like to go to university*

LA PUBLICIDAD

¿Dónde se encuentra la publicidad? Where do you find advertising?

la	cartelera	hoarding
el	catálogo	catalogue
la	columna anunciadora	advertising pillar
el	periódico	newspaper
la	radio	radio
la	revista	magazine
la	televisión	television

Palabras generales General

el	alquiler	hiring, hire
los	anuncios	small ads
la	bicicleta	bike
la	bicicleta de montaña	mountain bike
la	boda	marriage
el	buen precio	good value
la	casa	house
la	casa de vacaciones	holiday home
el	coche	car
el	eslogan publicitario	advertising slogan
el	fallecimiento	death
la	frescura	freshness
el	juego de palabras	pun, play on words
la	liquidación	sale
el	piso	flat
el	nacimiento	birth
el	placer	pleasure
los	precios bajos	low prices
los	productos	products
la	recompensa	reward
el	tiempo perdido	waste of time
las	vacaciones	holidays
el	valor	value
la	velocidad	speed

Adjetivos Adjectives

barato(a)	cheap
buen precio	good value (price)
divertido(a)	amusing
flamante	brand new
instructivo(a)	instructive
interesante	interesting
menos caro(a)	less expensive
nuevo(a)	new
mucho por poco	a lot for little
tonto(a)	stupid
útil	useful

se alquila	for hire
de segunda mano	second hand
precio negociable	price negotiable
en oferta	on offer
en los saldos	in the sales
se vende	for sale

A mi parecer In my opinion

Lo encuentro aburrido	I find it boring
Lo encuentro divertido	I find it funny
Me enfada	It makes me angry
Me hace reír	It makes me laugh
Me pone los nervios de punta	It gets on my nerves

Verbos útiles Useful verbs

alquilar	to rent, hire
aprovecharse de	to take advantage of
cambiar	to exchange
comprar	to buy
crear el deseo	to create a desire
investigar	to research
ofrecer	to offer
perder (ie)	to lose
recuperar	to find again, get back
vender	to sell

LLAMANDO POR TELÉFONO

Palabras generales General

el auricular .... earpiece, receiver
la cabina .... call box
el contestador automático
    .... answering machine
el correo electrónico .. e-mail
el fax .... fax machine
la guía .... directory
la información .... directory enquiries
la llamada de urgencia ..... an emergency call
la llamada telefónica .... phone call
la moneda .... coin
el número .... figure, number
el número de dos cifras ..... two figure number
el número de fax .... fax number
el número equivocado .... wrong number
el prefijo .... code
la tarifa .... rate, charge
la tarjeta telefónica .... phonecard
el/la telefonista .... operator
el teléfono móvil .... mobile phone
el teléfono público ..... payphone
el tono .... dialling tone
el usuario .... caller

a cobro revertido .... transferred charge
Espere el tono .... Wait for the dialling tone
Está communicando ..... The line's engaged
estropeado .... out of order
Marque el 061 .... Dial 061 (Ambulance)
Marque el 080 .... Dial 080 (Fire)
Marque el 091 .... Dial 091 (Police)
No cuelgue .... Hold the line

ocupado .... busy, engaged
la ranura .... slot

Dígame .... Hello (on the phone)
Soy yo .... "It's me" (on the phone)

¿Dónde puedo obtener una tarjeta telefónica?
Where can I get a phonecard?

en correos .... at the post office
en el estanco .... at the tobacconist's
en el quiosco .... at the news stand

Verbos útiles   Useful verbs

colgar (ue) .... to hang up
comprar .... to buy
cortarse .... to be cut off
darse .... to provide oneself with
dejar un recado .... to leave a message
descolgar (ue) .... to lift the handset
escuchar .... to listen
hablar .... to speak
llamar .... to call
llamar a cobro revertido
    ....to make a transferred charge call
llamar por teléfono .... to phone
marcar el número .... to dial the number
no figurar en la guía .... to be ex-directory
preguntar .... to ask
sonar (ue) .... to ring (of bell)
tener el teléfono .... to be on the phone
volver (ue) a llamar ..... to call back

Algunas frases

¿Dónde están las guías telefónicas? *Where are the phone books?*

Están al lado de las cabinas *They are next to the phone booths*

¿Es un teléfono de tarjeta? *Is it a cardphone?*

Buenos días. Quiero hablar con David, por favor *Hello, may I speak to David, please?*

Soy David *David speaking*

¿Quiere dejar un recado? *Would you like to leave a message?*

Te llaman al teléfono *You are wanted on the phone*

Para llamar al Reino Unido, marque el 07 44, luego el prefijo de la región sin el cero, y luego el número de la persona que llama *To phone the UK, dial 07 44, then the area code without the 0, and then the number of the person you are calling*

EL DINERO

Palabras generales General

el billete .... note

el dinero .... money

el dinero personal ...... pocket money

la moneda suelta .... cash

la moneda .... currency, coin

el banco .... bank

la Bolsa .... Stock Exchange

la caja de ahorros .... savings bank

el cajero automático... cash dispenser, cash point

el cambio .... change, exchange

el coste de la vida ...... cost of living

la hipoteca .... mortgage

la inflación .... inflation

el préstamo .... loan

el presupuesto .... budget

el cheque .... cheque

el cheque de viajero ... travellers' cheque

la cuenta corriente ..... current account

la cuenta de ahorros ... savings account

el eurocheque .... Eurocheque

el número personal de identificación .... PIN number

el talonario .... cheque book

la tarjeta del banco .... banker's card

la tarjeta de crédito.... credit card

el tipo de cambio .... exchange rate

Las monedas   **Currencies**

el balboa................... balboa

el bolívar.................. bolívar

el boliviano .... boliviano

el colón .... colón

el córdoba .... córdoba

el dólar..................... dollar

el guaraní .... guaraní

la lempira .... lempira

la libra esterlina......... £, pound sterling

la libra irlandesa........ Punt, Irish pound

la peseta .... peseta

el peso...................... peso

el sol .... sol

el sucre..................... sucre

el bolívar.................. bolívar

Verbos útiles   **Useful verbs**
ahorrar .... to save up
cambiar .... to change
comprar .... to buy
estar en números rojos . to be in the red
gastar dinero .... to spend money

pagar .... to pay (back)
pedir (i) prestado .... to borrow
prestar .... to lend
ser moneda corriente ... to be legal tender
valer .... to be worth

LAS VACACIONES Y LAS EXCURSIONES

Palabras generales General

el   día .... day
la   fiesta nacional .... national holiday
la   fecha .... date
el   invierno .... winter
el   mes .... month
la   noche .... night
el   otoño .... autumn
la   primavera .... spring
la   semana .... week
el   verano .... summer

El turismo   Tourism

el   almuerzo .... picnic
la   caminata .... long walk
la   colonia de verano (infantil)
     .... summer camp (children)
la   estancia .... stay
la   excursión .... outing
la   excursión escolar ... school trip
el   intercambio .... exchange
la   media pensión .... half board
el   parque de atracciones
     .... funfair, amusement park
el   parque de fieras ...... safari park
el   parque nacional ...... national park
el   paseo .... walk
la   pensión completa ... full board

el   precio .... price
la   región .... region
el   silencio .... silence
la   travesía .... crossing
las vacaciones .... holidays
el   viaje .... journey

el   aeropuerto .... airport
el   agente de viajes ..... travel agent
el   albergue juvenil ..... youth hostel
el   apartamento .... self-catering flat
el   banco .... bank
el   cambio .... exchange (currency)
el   camping .... camp site
la   casita .... self-catering cottage
el   centro de información ... information office
la   estación .... station
la   estación de autocares .... coach station
el   hotel .... hotel
la   oficina de turismo .. information office
la   pensión .... boarding house
el   puerto .... port

la   cámara de vídeo ..... camcorder
la   caravana .... caravan
el   carnet .... membership card
el   carnet de identidad .... identity card
el   cheque de viajero .... traveller's cheque
el   folleto .... brochure

la	foto.......................	photo
la	maleta....................	case
el	mapa de la región...	map of the region
la	máquina fotográfica....	camera
la	mochila..................	rucksack
el	pasaporte	passport
el	plano de la ciudad..	town plan
la	tienda....................	tent

La gente　　　People

el/la camarero(a)..........	waiter
el/la campista..............	camper
el/la conductor(a) de autocar....	coach driver
el/la dependiente(a)	sales assistant
el/la dueño(a)..............	owner
el/la guarda..................	youth hostel warden
la persona responsable....	group leader
el/la recepcionista........	receptionist
el/la salvavidas	lifeguard
el/la turista..................	tourist
los veraneantes	holiday makers
el/la vigilante..............	lifeguard

El alojamiento　　Lodging

El intercambio escolar
　　　　　　Going on an exchange

el	amigo de intercambio ...	penfriend
la	familia española.....	Spanish family
la	familia inglesa	English family
el/la profesor(a)		teacher

las	clases....................	lessons
el	colegio..................	school
la	comida..................	food
la	comida española	Spanish cooking
la	comida inglesa	English cooking
los	deberes	homework
los	deportes	sports
el	dinero personal	pocket money
la	duración................	length (stay, lesson)
la	excursión	outing
el	programa de estudio....	course of study
el	tiempo libre	free time

el	uniforme escolar....	school uniform
el	viaje	journey

comparar.....................	to compare
contrastar	to contrast

El albegue juvenil　　Youth hostel

el	agua caliente..........	hot water
la	cocina...................	kitchen
el	comedor	dining room
el	cubo de basura.......	rubbish bin
el	dormitorio	dormitory
la	manta	blanket
la	oficina	office
la	ropa......................	linen
el	saco-manta	sheet sleeping bag
la	sala (de día)	day room

El camping　　　Campsite

el	agua (no) potable...	(non) drinking water
el	alquiler de bicicletas ...	cycle hire
el	barreño	washing bowl
la	bombona (de gas) ..	gas cyclinder
la	cama de campaña...	camp bed
el	camping................	campsite, camping
la	caravana	caravan
el	carnet de camping..	camping carnet
las	cerillas..................	matches
la	cocina de gas	gas cooker
la	comida..................	food
la	comida para llevar	take-away meals
la	conexión eléctrica.........	electric hook-up
la	electricidad...........	electricity
el	enchufe.................	power point
el	equipo de camping........	camping equipment
el	fregadero	washing up sink
la	hoguera de campamento ...	camp fire
la	lavadora................	washing machine
la	lavandería..............	laundry
la	linterna	torch
la	navaja...................	pocket knife
la	piscina (de agua caliente)
	....	(heated) swimming pool

la piscina al aire libre. open air pool
la piscina cubierta ...... indoor pool
la recepción .... reception
la ropa sucia .... washing (clothes)
el saco de dormir .... sleeping bag
la sala de juegos........ games room
los servicios................ toilet block
el suplemento .... supplement
el terreno .... pitch
la tienda.................... tent
el vehículo................ vehicle

En un hotel   **At a hotel**
el aparcamiento .... car park
el ascensor................ lift
el baño...................... bath
la cama .... bed
la cama de matrimonio ...double bed
el cuarto de baño .... bathroom
la ducha.................... shower
la entrada.................. entrance
la escalera................. stairs
la ficha .... form
la habitación .... room
la habitación doble..... double room
la habitación familiar.....family room
la llave...................... key
el piso....................... storey, floor
la planta baja .... ground floor
el precio.................... price
la recepción .... reception
el restaurante .... restaurant
la salida (de urgencia) ....(emergency) exit
los servicios................ toilets
el sótano .... basement
el televisor................ TV set

la almohada .... pillow
el armario .... wardrobe
el jabón..................... soap
la manta.................... blanket
la percha................... coathanger
la sábana................... sheet

el teléfono .... telephone
la toalla .... towel

¿Para cuánto tiempo? For how long?
el día .... day
el mes....................... month
la noche.................... night
la semana .... week

para cuatro noches....... for four nights
para tres días .... for three days
para dos semanas........ for a fortnight

¿Para cuántas personas?   For how many?
el adulto .... adult
la chica..................... girl
el chico..................... boy
el/la niño(a) .... child
la persona................. person
menores de tres años.... under threes

For numbers see page 90
For other family words see page 26
For countries, towns, regions see page 88
For how to express opinions see page 38

¿Cuándo fuiste?   When did you go?
anteayer...................... the day before
                      yesterday
el año pasado.............. last year
ayer .... yesterday
durante el fin de semana ...during the weekend
hace dos meses .... two months ago
hace quince días .... a fortnight ago
la semana pasada .... last week

¿Cuándo vas?   When will you be going?
durante las vacaciones de verano
              ....during the summer holidays
el año que viene........... next year
en agosto .... in August
en Navidad .... at Christmas
en Pascua .... at Easter
en tres meses .... in three months' time
en una semana............. in a week's time

mañana........................ tomorrow
pasado mañana .... the day after tomorrow
la semana que viene... next week

¿Con quién?   **With whom?**
el amigo(a) .... friend
el amigo(a) de intercambio ...penfriend
la familia .... family

¿Qué comiste?   **What did you eat?**
la comida china .... Chinese food
la comida española .... Spanish cooking, food
la comida india .... Indian food

los caracoles .... snails
el chucrut................... sauerkraut
el crep salado............. savoury pancake
el curry...................... curry
la ensalada de Niza .... salade niçoise
el estafado de vaca..... beef casserole
la fabada asturiana ..... casserole of meat and
                              beans
el gazpacho............... cold, spicy vegetable
                              soup
la hamburguesa......... hamburger
los mariscos .... sea food
el pato a la naranja..... duck with orange sauce
la pechuga de pato ..... breast of duck
el pisto gallego .... mixed vegetables with
                              egg
el pollo en vino tinto.. coq au vin
la salsa de menta........ mint sauce
la sopa de cebolla ...... onion soup
la sopa de pescado ..... fish soup
la tarta de manzana .... apple tart
la terrina de hígado de pato
    .... duck liver terrine
las tortitas .... pancakes

For recipe words see page 55
For other foods see pages 23, 53

En la costa   **At the seaside**
el aceite bronceador... sun oil
la arena..................... sand
el bikini.................... bikini

el bote de remos .... rowing boat
la cabaña de playa ..... beach hut
la caña de pescar .... fishing rod
la caseta de primeros auxilios
    .... first aid post
el castillo de arena..... sandcastle
el cinturón salvavidas .... lifebelt
las conchas................. shells
el cubo .... bucket
las gafas de sol............ sunglasses
la gaviota................... seagull
los guijarros .... shingle
el helado................... ice cream
la lancha................... dinghy
la lancha inflable .... inflatable dinghy
la lancha motora........ motor boat
el mar....................... sea
la ola .... wave (sea)
la pala .... spade
la pamela.................. sunhat
el patín a pedales .... pedalo
la piscina.................. swimming pool
la plancha de windsurf.... sailboard
la playa..................... beach
la playa (no) vigilada..... (un)supervised beach
el traje de baño.......... swimsuit
la tumbona .... sunbed
el/la vendedor(a) de helados... ice cream seller
el yate (de arena)....... sand yacht

el acantilado.............. cliff
la bajamar .... low tide
la barca de pesca .... (fishing) boat
el faro....................... lighthouse
el muelle .... quay
el/la pescador(a) .... fisherman/woman
la pleamar .... high tide
el puerto................... port
el puerto deportivo .... yacht marina
el velero .... sailing ship
el yate .... yacht

Los deportes de invierno
Winter sports

La gente   **People**

el/la esquiador(a) .... skier
el/la guía .... guide
el/la monitor(a) .... ski instructor
el/la novato(a) .... beginner

La estación de esquí   **Ski resort**

el alud .... avalanche
la bola de nieve .... snowball
el chalé .... chalet
el copo de nieve .... snowflake
la montaña .... mountain
el muñeco de nieve .... snowman
la nevasca .... snowstorm
la nieve .... snow
la pista de esquí .... piste, ski run
la pista de patinaje ..... ice rink
el quitanieves .... snow-plough
el remolque T-bar ...... T-bar
el remonte .... ski lift
el teleférico .... cable car
el telesilla .... chair lift
la tienda de esquí .... ski shop

El equipo de esquí   **Skiing equipment**

el bastón de esquiar ... ski pole
las botas de esquí .... ski boots
el esquí .... ski
el gorro .... hat
el guante .... glove
los pantalones de\esquí .... ski pants
el peto de esquiar .... salopette

Las excursiones   Outings

El parque de fieras   **Safari park**

el animal .... animal
la cara .... face (animal)
la cola .... tail
el pájaro .... bird
la pata .... paw
el pez .... fish

el reptil .... reptile
la trompa .... trunk
la zarpa .... claw

la ballena .... whale
el camello .... camel
la cebra .... zebra
el chimpancé .... chimpanzee
el cocodrilo .... crocodile
el elefante .... elephant
la foca .... seal
la jirafa .... giraffe
el león .... lion
el lobo .... wolf
el mono .... monkey
la nutria .... otter
el oso .... bear
el oso blanco .... polar bear
el rinoceronte .... rhinoceros
la serpiente .... snake
el tigre .... tiger

La granja y el bosque   **Farm and woodland**

el campo .... field
la cuadra .... stable
el granero .... barn

la ardilla .... squirrel
el burro .... donkey
el caballo .... horse
la cabra .... goat
el cerdo .... pig
el conejo .... rabbit
el cordero .... lamb
el erizo .... hedgehog
la gallina .... hen
el gallito .... cockerel
el ganso .... goose
el gato .... cat
el novillo .... bullock
la oveja .... sheep
el pato .... duck
el pavo .... turkey
el perro .... dog

el pollo .... chicken
la rana .... frog
la rata .... rat
el ratón .... mouse
el sapo .... toad
la ternera .... calf
el toro....................... bull
la vaca...................... cow
el zorro..................... fox

For insects see page 86

El picnic   **Picnic**
¿Adónde vas?   **Where are you going?**
a la playa .... to the beach
a las montañas .... to the mountains
área de descanso .... picnic area
en el bosque................. in the forest
en el campo .... in the country

For weather see page 48
For food and drink for a picnic see page 53

¿Cómo era?   **What was it like?**
barato(a) .... cheap
bonito(a)..................... pretty
cómodo(a) .... comfortable
de lujo .... luxurious
disponible................... available
espléndido(a).............. superb
fantástico(a)................ fantastic
grande .... big
hermoso(a) .... beautiful
histórico(a) .... historic
incluido(a).................. included
industrial(a) .... industrial
lleno(a)...................... full
muy cómodo(a) .... very comfortable
no incluido(a) .... not included
obigatorio(a)............... compulsory
ocupado(a).................. taken
otro(a) .... other
para llevar .... take-away
pintoresco(a)............... pictureque

privado(a).................... private
prohibido(a) .... not allowed
ruidoso(a)................... noisy
soleado(a)................... sunny
sombreado(a) .... shady
sosegado(a) .... peaceful
todo el año .... all year round
tranquilo(a) .... peaceful
turístico(a).................. popular with tourists

Verbos útiles   **Useful verbs**
abrir .... to open
agradecer.................... to thank
andar .... to walk
ayudar .... to help
bañar(se) .... to bathe
buscar......................... to look for
caminar .... to walk
cerrar (ie) .... to close
costar (ue) .... to cost
dar un paseo .... to go for a walk
esquiar........................ to ski
estar de vacaciones...... to be on holiday
ir .... to go
nadar .... to swim
pagar.......................... to pay (for)
pasar dos semanas .... to spend a fortnight
ponerse en camino....... to set out
quedar(se) .... to stay
visitar......................... to visit

acampar...................... to camp
ahogar .... to drown
alquilar....................... to hire, let
caminar .... to go for a hike
cocinar .... to cook
dar un paseo en barco.. to go out in a boat
flotar .... to float
hacer alpinismo .... to go mountain
                   climbing
hacer camping............. to go camping
hacer esquí acuático .... to water ski

hacer esquí de fondo .... to do cross country ski-ing
hacer surf .... to surf
hacer vela .... to sail
hacer windsurf .... to sailboard
ir de vacaciones .... to go on holiday
ir en trineo .... to go sledging
jugar (ue) .... to play
marearse .... to be seasick
montar a caballo .... to ride (horse)
pasarlo bien .... to have a good time

poner una tienda .... to pitch a tent
remar .... to row
salir en avión .... to leave by plane
tirarse al agua .... to dive
tomar el almuerzo .... to take a picnic
tomar el sol .... to sunbathe
ver .... to see
veranear .... to take a summer holiday
viajar .... to travel
visitar .... to visit (place)

Algunas frases

Pasé las vacaciones de verano en la costa *I spent the summer holidays by the sea*

El año pasado visité Alemania *I visited Germany last year*

Hicimos camping en Francia *We went camping in France*

Fui con mi familia *I went with my family*

Pasamos dos semanas en las montañas *We spent a fortnight in the mountains*

Voy a España durante las vacaciones de Pascua *I shall be going to Spain in the Easter holidays*

En Navidades voy a esquiar en Andorra *I shall be going skiing in Andorra at Christmas*

Quisiera reservar una habitación con baño para dos personas *I would like to reserve a room, with a bath, for two people*

Queremos quedarnos tres noches *We are planning to stay three nights*

¿A qué hora se sirve el desayuno? *What time is breakfast?*

¿Dónde puedo aparcar el coche, por favor? *Where may I park the car, please?*

¿Hay un restaurante cerca del hotel? *Is there a restaurant near the hotel?*

No queda jabón *There is no soap left*

EL MUNDO INTERNACIONAL

Palabras generales General

los países desarrollados developed countries
los países en desarrollo developing countries
los países industrializados
.... industrialised countries
los países ricos .... rich countries
el tercer mundo.......... the third world

la agresión .... aggression
el analfabetismo......... illiteracy
el asilo político .... political asylum
el capitalismo .... capitalism
el color de la piel .... skin colour
el comercio a gran escala .. big business
el comunismo .... communism
la corrupción .... corruption
la enfermedad .... illness
la enfermedad psiquiátrica
.... psychiatric illness
la escasez................... poverty
la igualdad................. equality
la ley de la selva .... law of the jungle
la opinión política...... political opinion
la pobreza................. poverty (destitution)
la policía secreta .... secret police
el prejuicio .... prejudice
la religión .... religion
el/la sin hogar............. homeless person
el socialismo............. socialism

Verbos útiles Useful verbs

dar asilo a .... to give asylum to
explotar .... to exploit
matar .... to kill
respetar....................... to have respect for
suicidarse.................... to commit suicide
tolerar........................ to have tolerance for
torturar .... to torture

La historia y la política
History and politics

La gente   People

el/la diputado(a) .... MP
el/la presidente(a) .... president
el primer ministro...... prime minister
la primera ministra .... prime minister
la princesa .... princess
el príncipe .... prince
la reina .... queen
el rey .... king

la clase media............ middle class
la clase obrera .... working class
las Cortes................... Spanish parliament
la democracia .... democracy
el estado .... state
el franquismo .... period/system of
                General Franco (1939 - 1975)
el gobierno .... government
la guerra .... war
la Guerra Civil Española
.... the Spanish Civil War (1936 - 1939)
la guerra civil .... civil war
la monarquía .... monarchy
la nación................... nation
la opinión pública...... public opinion
el país........................ country
el parlamento............ parliament
el partido (político).... party (political)
la paz........................ peace
la Primera Guerra Mundial ... World War 1
la república............... republic
la revolución .... revolution
la Segunda Guerra Mundial .. World War 2
el socialismo .... socialism
el terrorismo............. terrorism

La geografía Geography

el acantilado .... cliff
la aldea .... village
el canal .... canal
la colina.................... hill
el continente .... continent
la llanura .... plain
la meseta................... plateau
la montaña................. mountain
el país .... country
el pico....................... peak
la provincia............... province
el pueblo................... town; village
el puerto .... mountain pass
la región .... region
el río......................... river
la sierra..................... mountain range
el valle...................... valley

La conservación Conservation

el espacio.................. space
el futuro.................... future
la luna....................... moon
el mundo .... world
la naturaleza .... nature
el planeta .... planet
el sol......................... sun
la tierra..................... earth

las aves .... bird life
el bosque .... forest
la capa de ozono .... ozone layer
el clima ecuatorial ..... equatorial climate
el clima polar............. polar climate
el clima templado ...... temperate climate
el clima tropical......... tropical climate
el ecosistema .... ecosystem
el equilibrio natural .. natural balance
la fauna..................... animals, fauna
la flora...................... flora
la hoja....................... leaf
el medio ambiente ..... environment

la naturaleza salvaje... wilderness
las plantas .... plants
la vida marina............ marine life

Los desastres Disasters

el alud .... avalanche .
el cambio de clima .... change in climate
la contaminación urbana... urban pollution
la deforestación .... deforestation
el deshielo .... thawing
el efecto invernadero .... greenhouse effect
la epidemia...................... epidemic
la erupción volcánica........ volcanic eruption
los estragos de la polución.. ravages of pollution
la explosión .... explosion
la falta de lluvia......... lack of rain
la guerra .... war
el hambre (f) .... famine
el incendio................. fire
la inundación............. flood
el maremoto .... tidal wave
la sequía .... drought
el terremoto.............. earthquake
el tornado .... tornado

Las fuentes de contaminación Sources of pollution

el ácido..................... acid
el camión cisterna de gas.....gas tanker
el carbón .... coal
la central eléctrica ..... power station
la central nuclear .... nuclear power station
el combustible .... fuel
el combustible fósil ... fossil fuels
la escombrera .... slag heap
la fábrica .... factory
el gas natural .... natural gas
los gases de escape...... exhaust gases
la industria del carbón .... coal industry
las industrias químicas ..... chemical industries
la lluvia ácida .... acid rain
la madera.................. wood

85

la   mancha de petróleo..... oil on beach
la   marea negra........... oil slick
el   pesticida................ pesticide
el   petrolero................ oil tanker
el   polvo radiactivo..... radio-active fall-out
la   refinería de petróleo....oil refinery
el   tráfico................... traffic
el   tubo de escape .... exhaust pipe

Los deshechos domésticos
Domestic waste

la   lata de aluminio ..... aluminium can
la   lata de acero........... steel can
el   metal..................... metal
el   papel..................... paper
el   plástico.................. plastic
el   reciclaje................. recycling waste
el   vidrio.................... glass

claro .... clear
marrón......................... brown
verde .... green

La fauna   Fauna
Los insectos   Insects
la   abeja..................... bee
la   araña..................... spider
la   avispa .... wasp
la   hormiga .... ant
la   mariposa .... butterfly
la   mariposa nocturna.. moth
la   mariquita .... ladybird
la   mosca .... fly
el   mosquito............... mosquito
la   oruga .... caterpillar

Las aves   Birds
el   ave migratoria (f)... migratory bird
las   aves acuáticas .... waterfowl
las   aves rapaces........... birds of prey
el   cisne .... swan
el   cóndor .... condor
la   lechuza .... barn owl

Las especies en peligro
Endangered species
la   ballena azul .... blue whale
el   delfín.................... dolphin
el   orangután .... orang-utan
el   oso blanco .... polar bear
el   panda.................... giant panda
el   tiburón.................. shark

For other animals see page 81

el   cadáver.................. corpse
el   colmillo................. tusk
el   hábitat .... habitat
el   marfil .... ivory
la   piel .... fur
el   pienso................... fodder
el   plancton................ plankton

La flora   Flora
el   abeto..................... fir tree
el   árbol..................... tree
el   bosque.................. wood
la   flor .... flower
las   flores silvestres...... wild flowers
el   jacinto silvestre...... bluebell
el   olmo..................... elm
el   pino .... pine tree
la   pluviselva .... rain forest
la   primavera .... primrose
el   roble..................... oak
la   selva .... forest

Adjetivos   Adjectives
fatal............................ awful
herido(a) .... injured, wounded
caliente....................... hot
criminal...................... criminal
del norte .... northern
ecológico(a) .... ecological
escarpado(a) .... steep
frío(a)........................ cold
húmedo(a) .... humid, wet

irreversible .... irreversible
lluvioso(a) .... wet
nuboso(a)..................... cloudy, overcast
nuclear....................... nuclear
oscuro(a) .... dark, gloomy
químico(a) .... chemical
ruidoso(a) .... noisy
suave .... soft, gentle
templado(a) .... mild, lukewarm
urbano(a)..................... urban

Verbos útiles   **Useful verbs**
amenazar .... to threaten
bajar .... to fall (temperature)
condenar..................... to condemn, doom
conservar.................... to conserve, protect
contaminar.................. to pollute
cultivar .... to grow, cultivate
despojar..................... to despoil

destrozar..................... to destroy
envenenar.................... to poison
escoger...................... to pick
exceder...................... to exceed
extender .... to spread
limitar el daño .... to limit the damage
limpiar los tanques ...... to flush out tanks
matar........................ to kill
mejorar...................... to improve
producir un clima .... to produce a climate
quemar .... to burn, parch
respirar...................... to breathe
robar......................... to steal
secar......................... to parch, dry out
sospechar................... to suspect
subir......................... to rise (temperature)
sufrir .... to suffer
verter en el mar .... to dump at sea
                                (oil, chemicals)

LOS PAÍSES, LAS REGIONES, LAS CIUDADES

La Unión Europea　　　　**The European Union**

País Country	Meaning	Idioma Language	Gentilicio Inhabitant	Adjetivo Adjective
Inglaterra	England	el inglés	un(a) inglés/esa	inglés
Escocia	Scótland	el inglés	un(a) escocés/esa	escocés
Irlanda del Norte	N Ireland	el inglés	un(a) irlandés/esa	irlandés
Irlanda	Irish Republic	el irlandés, el inglés	un(a) irlandés/esa	irlandés
Gales	Wales	el galés, el inglés	un(e) galés/esa	galés
Alemania	Germany	el alemán	un(a) alemán/ana	alemán
Austria	Austria	el alemán	un(a) austríaco(a)	austríaco
Bélgica	Belgium	el francés, el flamenco	un(a) belga	belga
Dinamarca	Denmark	el danés	un(a) danés/esa	danés
España	Spain	el español	un(a) español(a)	español
Finlandia	Finland	el finlandés	un(a) finlandés/esa	finlandés
Francia	France	el francés	un(a) francés/esa	francés
Grecia	Greece	el griego	un(a) griego(a)	griego
Italia	Italy	el italiano	un(a) italiano(a)	italiano
Luxemburgo	Luxembourg	el francés, el alemán	un(a) luxemburgués/esa	luxemburgués
los Países Bajos	Netherlands	el holandés	un(a) holandés/esa	holandés
Portugal	Portugal	el portugués	un(a) portugués/esa	portugués
Suecia	Sweden	el sueco	un(a) sueco(a)	sueco

Los países hispanohablantes

(la) Argentina .... Argentina
Bolivia .... Bolivia
Chile .... Chile
Colombia .... Colombia
Costa Rica .... Costa Rica
Cuba .... Cuba
(el) Ecuador .... Ecuador
Filipinas .... the Philippines
Guatemala .... Guatemala
la Guayana .... Guyana
Honduras .... Honduras
Marruecos .... Morocco
Méjico .... Mexico
Nicaragua .... Nicaragua
(el) Panamá .... Panama

(el) Paraguay .... Paraguay
(el) Perú .... Peru
Puerto Rico .... Puerto Rico
(la) República Dominicana
.... Dominican Republic
El Salvador .... El Salvador
(el) Uruguay .... Uruguay
Venezuela .... Venezuela

Otros países　　　**Other countries**

(el) África del Sur .... South Africa
América .... America
las Antillas .... West Indies
Australia .... Australia
Bangladesh .... Bangladesh
(el) Brasil .... Brazil

88

(la) China .... China
Granada .... Grenada
(la) India .... India
las Islas Bermudas .... Bermuda
Jamaica .... Jamaica
(el) Japón .... Japan
Noruega .... Norway
Nueva Zelanda............. New Zealand
(el) Paquistán .... Pakistan
Rusia .... Russia
Tailandia .... Thailand
(el) Vietnam .... Vietnam

Algunas regiones Regions

Cornualles............. Cornwall
las Islas Anglonormandas... Channel Islands
las Islas Sorlingues...... Isles of Scilly
las Órcadas................. Orkney Isles

Las Coomunidades Autónomas de España
Spanish Autonomous Communities
Andalucía .... Andalusia
Aragón .... Aragon
Asturias .... Asturias
Cantabria .... Cantabria
Castilla-La Mancha...... Castile-La Mancha
Castilla y León .... Castile and Leon
Cataluña .... Catalonia
Ceuta .... Ceuta
Galicia....................... Galicia
(las) Islas Baleares....... Balearic Islands
(las) Islas Canarias....... Canary Islands
Madrid....................... Madrid
Melilla....................... Melilla
Murcia....................... Murcia
Navarra...................... Navarre
(el) País Vasco .... Basque Country
La Rioja..................... La Rioja
Valencia .... Valencia

Algunas ciudades Some towns

Bogotá....................... Bogota
Bruselas..................... Brussels
Cantórbery .... Canterbury
Córdoba .... Cordova
Edimburgo .... Edinburgh
Ginebra .... Geneva
La Haya...................... The Hague
Lisboa .... Lisbon
Londres...................... London
Moscú .... Moscow
Nueva York................. New York
París......................... Paris
Sevilla....................... Seville
Zaragoza .... Saragossa

Los mares, las montañas y los ríos Seas, mountains and rivers

el Canal de la Mancha ..... English Channel
el Estrecho de Dover .... Straits of Dover
el Mar Báltico .... Baltic Sea
el Mar de Irlanda ...... Irish Sea
el Mar del Norte .... North Sea
el Mar Mediterráneo.. Mediterranean Sea
el Mar Muerto .... Dead Sea
el Mar Negro............ Black Sea
el Mar Rojo.............. Red Sea
el Océano Atlántico... Atlantic Ocean
el Océano Pacífico..... Pacific Ocean

los Alpes.................... Alps
los Andes .... Andes
los Pirineos .... Pyrenees

el Canal de Panamá ... Panama Canal
el Duero .... Duero
el Ebro .... Ebro
el Guadalquivir......... Guadalquivir
el Guadiana .... Guadiana
el Mino.................... Mino
el Orinico .... Orinico
el Río de la Plata .... River Plate
el Tajo..................... Tajo
el Támesis .... Thames

LOS NÚMEROS, LA HORA Y LA FECHA

Los números cardinales		Cardinal numbers			
0	cero	20	veinte	80	ochenta
1	uno	21	veintiuno	81	ochenta y uno
2	dos	22	veintidós	82	ochenta y dos
3	tres	23	veintitrés	90	noventa
4	cuatro	24	veinticuatro	91	noventa y uno
5	cinco	25	veinticinco	92	noventa y dos
6	seis	26	veintiséis	100	cien
7	siete	27	veintisiete	101	ciento uno
8	ocho	28	veintiocho	105	ciento cinco
9	nueve	29	veintinueve	110	ciento diez
10	diez	30	treinta	150	ciento cincuenta
11	once	31	treinta y uno	300	trescientos
12	doce	40	cuarenta	308	trescientos ocho
13	trece	41	cuarenta y uno	400	cuatrocientos
14	catorce	50	cincuenta	406	cuatrocientos seis
15	quince	60	sesenta	1.000	mil
16	dieciséis	70	setenta	1.203	mil doscientos tres
17	diecisiete	71	setenta y uno	5.000	cinco mil
18	dieciocho	72	setenta y dos	1.000.000	un millón
19	diecinueve	79	setenta y nueve	1.000.000.000	mil millones (un billón)

La fecha   The date

Hoy es el primero de setiembre.................... Today is September 1st

Hoy es (el) dos de enero .... Today is January 2nd

Hoy es (el) ocho de marzo .... Today is March 8th

Hoy es (el) once de abril............................. Today is April 11th

Hoy es (el) diecinueve de mayo.................. Today is May 19th

Hoy es (el) catorce de julio......................... Today is July 14th

Mi cumpleaños es el diez de noviembre....... My birthday is November 10th

Nací en mil novecientos ochenta y dos .... I was born in 1982

Los números ordinales

primero(a) .... first
segundo(a) .... second
tercero(a) .... third
cuarto(a) .... fourth
quinto(a) .... fifth
sexto(a) .... sixth
séptimo(a) .... seventh
octavo(a) .... eighth
noveno(a) .... ninth
décimo(a) .... tenth
undécimo(a) .... eleventh
duodécimo(a)............... twelfth

Ordinal numbers

décimotercero(a) .... thirteenth
décimocuarto(a) .... fourteenth
décimoquinto(a) .... fifteenth
décimosexto(a) .... sixteenth
decimoséptimo(a) .... seventeenth
decimoctavo(a) .... eighteenth
decimonoveno(a) .... nineteenth
vigésimo(a) .... twentieth

Remember that ordinal numbers are **not** used in dates

La hora

Es la una.. It is one o'clock
Son las dos .... It is two o'clock
Son las tres y cinco .... It is five past three
Son las cuatro y diez.. It is ten past four
Son las cinco y cuarto.. It is quarter past five
Son las seis y veinte... It is twenty past six
Son las siete y veinticinco...................................... It is twenty five past seven
Son las ocho y media... It is half past eight
Son las dos menos veinticinco .... It is twenty five to two
Son las tres menos veinte.. It is twenty to three
Son las cuatro menos cuarto .... It is quarter to four
Son las cinco menos diez.. It is ten to five
Son las seis menos cinco.. It is five to six

Es mediodía.. It is midday, noon
Son las doce y cinco de la tarde .... It is five past twelve (midday)
Son las doce y cuarto.. It is quarter past twelve
Son las doce menos cuarto...................................... It is quarter to twelve
Es medianoche.. It is midnight
Son las doce y diez de la noche.............................. It is ten past twelve (night)
Son las doce y media de la noche........................... It is half past twelve (night)
Son las doce menos diez de la noche...................... It is ten to twelve (night)
Son las veinte horas 20.00
Son las veintidós quince 22.15
Son las dieciocho treinta.. 18.30
Son las trece cuarenta y cinco 13.45

Las partes del día

el día .... day
la madrugada .... early hours of the
                                morning
la mañana .... morning

Parts of the day

la noche .... night
la tarde .... afternoon, evening
todos los días .... every day

Los días de la semana

lunes .... Monday
martes .... Tuesday
miércoles .... Wednesday
jueves .... Thursday

Days of the week

viernes .... Friday
sábado .... Saturday
domingo .... Sunday

Los meses del año

enero .... January
febrero .... February
marzo .... March
abril .... April
mayo .... May
junio .... June

Months of the year

julio .... July
agosto .... August
setiembre .... September
octubre .... October
noviembre .... November
diciembre .... December

ABREVIATURAS Y SIGLAS

AA.EE. (Asuntos Exteriores) .... Foreign Office
a. de C. (antes de Cristo) .. .. BC
BUP (Bachillerato Unificado y Polivalente) .... GCSE equivalent
CA (Comunidad Autónoma) .... local government
CAMPSA (Compañía Arrendataria de Monopolio de Petróleo, SA) .... state petrol company
CAP (Certificado de Aptitud Pedagógica) .... teaching certificate
CE (Comisión de Europea) .... European Commission
CEOE (Confederación Española de Organizaciones Empresariales) .... CBI equivalent
CNT (Confederación Nacional de Trabajo) .... trade union
COE (Comité Olímpico Español) .... Spanish Olympic Committee
COU (Curso de Orientación Universitaria) .... pre-university year
CTNE (Compañía Telefónica Nacional de España) .... BT equivalent
DAO (Diseño Asistido por Ordenador) .... CAD
d.C. (después de Cristo) .... AD
EGB (Educación General Básica) .... primary/middle years education
EE.UU. (Estados Unidos). .... USA
ELE (Español como Lengua Extranjera) .... Spanish as a Foreign Language

ENDESA (Empresa Nacional de Electricidad, SA) .... Spanish electricity

ETS (enfermedad de transmisión sexual) .... STD (sexually transmitted disease)

FF.AA. (Fuerzas Armadas) .... Armed Forces

FOP (Fuerzas del Orden Público) .... security forces

FSE (Fondo Social Europeo) .... European Social Fund

IGN (Instituto Geográfico Nacional) .... National Geographical Institute

IPC (índice de precios al consumo) .... retail price index

ITV (Inspección Técnica de Vehículos) .... MOT

IVA (Impuesto de Valor Añadido) .... VAT

JJ.OO. (Juegos Olímpicos) .... Olympic Games

MCE (Mercado Común Europeo) .... European Common Market

ONU (Organización de las Naciones Unidas) .... UN

OTAN (Organización del Tratado del Atlántico Norte) ..... NATO

OVNI (Objeto Volador No Identificado) .... UFO

PNB (Producto Nacional Bruto) .... GNP (gross national product)

RNE (Radio Nacional de España) .... Spanish radio

PSOE (Partido Socialista Obrero Español) .... Spanish "Labour Party"

RENFE (Red Nacional de Ferrocarriles Españoles) .... Spanish railways

RTVE (Radiotelevisión Española) .... Spanish TV

SA (Sociedad Anónima) .... plc

SAR (Su Alteza Real) .... HRH (His/Her Royal Highness)

SEAT (Sociedad Española de Automóviles de Turismo) ... Spanish car manufacturer

SIDA (síndrome de inmuno-deficiencia adquirida) .... AIDS

SL (Sociedad Limitada) .... Ltd.

SM (Su Majestad) .... His/Her Majesty

SME (Sistema Monetario Europeo) .... European Monetary System

SMI (salario mínimo interprofesional) .... minimum wage

SRC (se ruega contestación) .... RSVP

ss (siguientes) .... following

Sr. (Señor) .... Mr

Sra. (Señora) .... Mrs, Ms

Srta. (Señorita) .... Miss, Ms

TAE (tasa anual efectiva) .... APR, annual percentage rate

TALGO (tren articulado ligero Goicoechea-Oriol) .... inter-city train

TAV (Tren de Alta Velocidad) .... high speed train

TER (Tren Español Rápido) .... inter-city express

UCP (unidad central de proceso) .... central processing unit (CPU)

UGT (Unión General de Trabajadores) .... trade union

UVI (Unidad de Vigilancia Intensiva) .... intensive care unit

VCL (visualizador de cristal líquido) .... LCD

VO (versión original) .... undubbed version of film

VPO (viviendas de protección oficial) .... council housing

NOTES

MALVERN LANGUAGE GUIDES

PO Box 76   Malvern   WR14 2YP   UK

Priceline/Fax: 01684 893756   Enquiries: 01684 577433

	French	German	Spanish	Italian	Total ordered	Price each	subtotal £
GCSE Vocabulary Guide						£2.50	
GCSE Speaking Test Guide						£2.50	
Grammar Guide						£3.50	
Dictionary						£3.50	
Key Stage 3 Guide						£3.00	
Standard Grade Vocabulary †						£2.50	
Comm. Entrance 13+ Guide						£3.50	
Mon échange scolaire						£2.00	
Mein Austausch						£2.00	
Mi intercambio escolar						£2.00	
Ma visite en France						£2.00	
My visit to Britain						£2.00	
*Sticker Pack A (192 stickers)						*£5.00	
*Mixed Sticker Pack A (192 stickers in four languages – 48 per language)						*£5.00	
*Multiplication Tables stickers (192 stickers)						*£5.00	
*Literacy Stickers (192 stickers in English)						*£5.00	
*Achievement Stickers (192 stickers in English)						*£5.00	
*Plastic library-style book cover (A5 format fits all our books)						*£0.50	
*Box of 100 plastic library-style book covers						*£35.00	
*Handling charge for orders totalling £3.99 or less						*£1.50	
						UK/EU Total	

Delivery charge for customers outside the European Union (EU) – add 30% of UK/EU total

* price includes VAT   † for Scotland   **TOTAL PAYABLE: £** _____

Name	
Address	
Postcode	**Telephone**

Terms: Strictly cheque payable to **Malvern Language Guides** with order. No coins please. We aim to despatch goods within 7 days of receipt of your order. We regret we are unable to accept orders over the phone or payment by credit card. For orders of £4 and over we make no charge for delivery to UK or EU addresses. Outside of the EU add 30% to the total cost of the order. **Prices valid to 31.7.99.** We can accept cheques in any EU currency, Swiss francs, US $, Australian $, NZ $, Canadian $, Hong Kong $, SA Rand. Republic of Ireland IR£1 = stg£1. Simply convert the total using rates in the press. For other currencies, please 'phone us.

Signed .... **Date** ....